I0539771

On the Green Earth
Contemplating
The Moon

MELISSA L. WHITE

Channing Way Press

San Francisco

Copyright © 2012 Melissa L. White

All rights reserved.

ISBN:0615730477
ISBN-13:978-0615730479

DEDICATION

For Terrence

You are the Sunshine of My Life

CONTENTS

"And I am here
On the green earth contemplating the moon
Much marveling what may betide tomorrow
I love my life."

From *"Manuscript Poems 1820-1829"*
                    Ralph Waldo Emerson

Angel Food

A warm breeze whispered through the half open window, stirring the vertical blinds and spreading the hot breath of the Santa Anna winds throughout the office. After watching the orientation DVD, Dana Brown glanced around at the cluttered office. Books and papers were piled upon every inch of surface space on all the bookshelves, desks, and counter tops. She licked her lips, realizing she was hungry as she savored the peppery thick aroma of turkey and cornbread dressing wafting overhead, making her mouth water. A gray-haired woman in a tie-dyed T-shirt and cut-offs approached.

"All finished?" she asked, giving Dana a clipboard and pen.

Dana nodded.

"Okay," said the woman. "After watching this DVD, are you still interested?"

"Absolutely. When can I start?"

The woman grinned and pointed at the clipboard. "That's our sign-up sheet, explaining our current openings. As you can see, we have more than enough drivers. What we really need right now is kitchen help."

She hesitated, sensing Dana's disappointment then added, "Actually, the kitchen crew is a lot of fun. It's the heart of our operation."

Dana nodded, offering a half smile.

"You can't imagine how many lives you'll touch."

Dana fiddled with her pen cap, wishing she could be a driver instead of a cook. She didn't relish the idea of being stuck in a hot crowded kitchen.

The woman smiled and said, "Standing over a hot stove has its own rewards too, you know, especially when you cook with love."

Studying the woman's face, Dana noticed the laugh lines reaching out from her eyes like creases in an often-read paperback book. Wisps of silvery hair framed her face and her soothing voice made Dana feel calm. Safe. Almost sleepy, as if rocked in a cradle.

"Obviously, in any volunteer meal delivery program, love should always be the main ingredient, don't you agree?"

The woman paused, waiting for Dana to respond.

Dana cleared her throat then said weakly, "I'm sorry, I forgot your name."

"Ernestine," she said, eyes sparkling.

She gave Dana an information booklet and asked her to take it home and read it. Dana glanced over the sign-up sheet again, but all the open time slots for kitchen help interfered with her work schedule during the week. And all the weekend slots were filled of course. Just as Ernestine began to explain a little about the founding of Project Angel Food, three teenage girls came marching in, lugging two large cardboard boxes. They dumped the boxes on the front desk.

Ernestine stood and called out to them, "Can I help you ladies?"

"Sorry," one of the girls said as she approached, "But it's almost three o'clock and we have to be home by 4:00."

"Are those the meals?" Ernestine asked.

The girls nodded. "We got totally lost. The directions are really mixed up. We couldn't follow them." She gave a folded up Mapquest printout to Ernestine.

The other girls approached timidly. "We're sorry," said the smallest girl. "But we're from Orange County and we don't know our way around Hollywood."

Ernestine waved it off. "No problem. How many meals did you deliver?"

"Two," said the smallest girl.

Ernestine sighed. "Oh well, thanks for trying."

The girls apologized again then hurried outside. Ernestine smoothed the wrinkled printout, glancing over the names. "Damn," she said under her breath.

"What route is it?" Dana asked.

Ernestine flipped the sheet over and read the route information. "Looks like Silverlake."

"I used to work there, so I know the area. I'd be glad to deliver those meals for you."

Ernestine grabbed Dana's hand. "Oh! Could you?"

"Absolutely."

"What a godsend you are, dear. What's your name again?"

"Dana Brown."

"You see, Dana? You wanted to be a driver, didn't you? So welcome to Project Angel Food's Route 26." Ernestine grabbed Dana's hands then hugged her. "I'm so glad you were sent to us."

Ernestine shoved the Mapquest directions into Dana's hand.

"I'll help you with these boxes," Ernestine said. "There are seventeen names on this route. Always make sure you deliver the correct lunch because some people have special meal plans. Like low sodium, or vegetarian, or whatever."

Ernestine and Dana carried the boxes to Dana's car. Ernestine double checked the list then said, "Number seven has a special menu. Make sure he gets the correct lunch. Also if no one's home, don't leave anything. Always bring it back. We have to respect our client's right to privacy. I mean these are AIDS patients. They've got enough to worry about. Okay?"

"Got it," said Dana, slipping in behind the wheel of her car.

"Good luck," said Ernestine. "And thanks so much. You're an angel."

Dana pulled onto Santa Monica Boulevard, wondering if she really was an angel. It was Saturday. Her husband, Brian, was home watching football on TV. And Dana had been meaning to volunteer for something, anything, it didn't matter what. Just so she could fill in that blank marked "community service" on her application for public relations manager at work. It would mean a promotion and a huge raise if she got the job. So here she was. But did this truly qualify her as an angel?

Dana opened her sunroof as she drove down Santa Monica Boulevard towards Echo Park. The air was crisp. Last night's rain had washed away the smog and dust. Once she reached Silverlake, she drove to Larissa Lane to deliver the first meal. No one answered the door but just as Dana started to leave, an old man peeked out of the window.

"Leave it on the porch please," he called through the open window then ducked back behind the sheer curtains.

"Sorry this is late," Dana said, watching his silhouette through the curtains.

He did not answer.

Dana hurried down the sidewalk to her car and when she glanced back at the front porch, the sack of food was gone.

The next five houses were on the same street. Each of these clients was very gracious and accepted Dana's apology for being late with the meals. They enjoyed having someone to talk to.

The seventh delivery was a little more involved. According to the instructions on the printout, Dana had to punch in a security code at the main entrance. She did this and the mammoth wooden gate buzzed open. She followed a steep stone stairway as it wound down the hill to a small cottage on a cliff overlooking the valley below. When she rang the doorbell, a voice spoke to her through an intercom beside the door.

"Who's there?"

"The driver from Project Angel Food." Dana leaned into the intercom. "Sorry your lunch is so late."

The door buzzed open and Dana stepped inside.

"Come in, come in. Don't be timid. I'm in here."

Dana peeked into the den and the room assaulted her senses. A lingering odor of diapers and Pine-Sol greeted her as the man said, "You're late."

Dana apologized, holding the sack lunch up like a peace offering. She tried not to stare at the masses of red fabric covering the walls and ceiling. Even his bed was canopied with the same bright red curtains. If she had not seen his gaunt cheeks and pale skin, she would have guessed she had entered the private harem quarters of an Arabian sheik.

The only break from the visual onslaught of red fabric was the large bay window, which drew Dana to its light. The view from the hill was marvelous, overlooking Los Feliz in the valley below.

"You can put it in the fridge. I'm not even hungry any more."

He pointed behind her, so Dana wandered into the kitchen and opened the fridge. It was empty except for a jar of applesauce and a half dozen plastic syringes.

When she returned to his room, the man said, "I hope they didn't mix it up again. I'm supposed to get a special meal plan, but the last three meals have been wrong."

Dana checked her list. "Low sodium diet with Ensure to drink."

"Well maybe it's right this time. It's just three hours late."

"So can I get you anything before I leave?" Dana asked over her shoulder, heading for the door.

"No, my nurse comes in the morning. And my mouth hurts so much I can't eat anything anyway. Wait a minute...."

Dana hesitated at the door, hoping he wouldn't prolong this visit. It never occurred to her that filling in that community service blank on her application might lead to something like this. Dana thought perhaps she should have stayed in the kitchen like Ernestine suggested. The pungent smell in this room was getting to her. She noticed her palms were sweating.

"I suppose you could bring me a pitcher of water. Look in the cupboard by the sink. The red pitcher. Just fill it up with water from the dispenser in the pantry."

Dana hurried back to the kitchen, found the pitcher and filled it up. She reached into the cabinet for a glass and a huge cockroach scurried away. She nearly screamed.

When she returned with the water, the man offered her twenty dollars if she would massage his feet. He said his medication caused muscle cramps and his feet were aching. He pointed to the chair at the foot of his bed.

"There's a twenty on the dresser," he said.

"That won't be necessary," Dana heard herself say as she inwardly cringed at the thought of touching this man's feet. Seeing no polite way to refuse, she sat beside his bed and began rubbing the arches of his feet.

"That feels so good," he said, "You just can't imagine."

Dana nodded. The soles of his feet were dry and rough and felt almost like stucco against her hands. She worked quickly and quietly and spent the next ten minutes listening to this perfect stranger tell her all about his throbbing joints and his unbearably painful mouth sores until she started feeling claustrophobic.

At last Dana told him that she hoped he had a better day tomorrow, but that she still had other deliveries to make so she should be going. She washed her hands in the kitchen before she left.

Climbing back up the steep winding pathway to the street, Dana could not shake the image of this man in his bed. Surely a simple vaccine could alleviate this kind of pain, Dana thought to herself. How much longer until a vaccine could be produced? And how many lives hung in the balance? As she reached her car, Dana looked down and saw that her hands were shaking. She wanted a beer, and she wanted to curl up next to her husband and fall asleep in front of the TV. Then she felt ashamed for being repulsed by that man's suffering.

Back in the safe haven of her Honda, Dana checked the list again. The next name on the itinerary was Stan MacGreggor.

Dana had gone to high school with a boy name Stan MacGreggor. He was gorgeous. All the girls adored him, but he never seemed to have a steady girlfriend. She wondered for a moment if this might be the same guy.

"No way," she told herself then imagined that the Stan MacGreggor she knew in school was probably still living in Texas with a wife and three kids, a patio home, and an SUV in the driveway.

She rang the bell then heard footsteps inside. When the door opened, Dana was completely taken aback. *It was him.* The same Stan MacGreggor she had known in high school. This was the same guy who had nicknamed her RAGU because her boyfriend, Jamey, had confided to him that Dana was a royal bitch when it was her time of the month. Although it had been years since high school graduation, she still felt embarrassed when she thought of being called Ragu, especially now, standing on Stan's front porch, holding a sack of turkey and dressing.

"Stan?" Dana said awkwardly.

He looked at her, unsure. "Yeah?"

"It's me, Dana."

He stared at her for a moment then Dana could see that old recognition in his eyes, but only briefly. He backed away as if discomfited.

"Look, I'm sorry the meal is so late, but the original driver got lost. I just happened to be at the kitchen, signing up as a new volunteer when the driver came back with all this food. So I said I knew the Silverlake area pretty well."

He stared down at his food.

"What an amazing coincidence," Dana blurted out, feeling her cheeks flush as soon as she said it. "I mean bumping into you here in L.A., of all places. I hope you're okay." She looked down at her feet, fumbling for the right words. "Listen, Stan. If there's anything you need, or anything at all I can help you with, please let met know."

He glanced back inside his house. Dana felt like an uninvited guest at a very private party.

"Okay? So I'll leave my number here with you. And you call me if you need a ride anywhere, or if you need someone to come take out the trash or clean house or help you with whatever you don't feel like doing." Dana reached into her jacket pocket and pulled out her wallet, looking for her business cards.

"Oh no. I'm all out of cards."

Stan watched her dig through her wallet until she found an old bank deposit slip. She pulled it out and offered it to him. "This has my phone number, you call me if you need anything. Okay?"

He hesitated then took the deposit slip and read it aloud. "Dana Brown and Brian O'Donnell?" He glanced up at Dana, smiling that 'Ultra-Brite' smile that once melted the hearts of many Texas girls. "Are you married now?" Stan asked.

"Yes," Dana said. "Eight years."

"You live in Marina del Rey?" he asked. "Nice place."

"Yes. It is," Dana said. "We live on a sailboat."

He looked up at her surprised. "Really?"

She nodded.

"Cool." He glanced back over his shoulder again then said, "So would you like to come in? Or do you have other meals to deliver?"

"Actually, I do have a few left." She checked her watch then laughed. "But they're already three hours late, what's a few more minutes."

Stan smiled. He stepped aside and held the door open for Dana to enter. She followed him into the living room.

"Have a seat," he said, pointing to the cushy futon by the window. He hurried into the kitchen and opened the louvered shutters at the bar separating the den from the kitchen. "Can I get you something to drink? Coke? Diet Coke? Cherry Coke?"

Dana laughed. "Coke is fine."

He carried in two cans of soda and two crystal champagne flutes, a blue glass plate and a blue linen napkin inside a golden half moon napkin ring.

"So you live on a sailboat. How interesting. Did you sail it here?"

Dana laughed. "No, we bought it here. It's our home. It was the most affordable way for us to live in the Marina. Plus Brian loves to sail."

Stan nodded then said, "So how long have you lived here?"

"Five years."

He took a sip of his Coke then said, "So what brings you to the City of Angels? Business or pleasure?"

"Work," Dana said. "Brian's a musician. He got a good offer from a band passing through Dallas where we used to live."

Stan carefully unwrapped the foil and examined the turkey and dressing. "Amazing. It's still warm."

"So Stan. What brings you here?"

He placed the food on his plate, then cut a sliver of white meat and dipped it into the gravy. "I did a little modeling in Dallas, until my agent bought me a one-way ticket to Hollywood three years ago. It was the best thing that ever happened to me. Until recently."

"Why? What happened?"

He looked at her and laughed. Seeing the confusion on her face, Stan held up his Project Angel Food lunch sack.

"Oh," Dana said, embarrassed. She stared at her drink. After an extended silence she said, "So do you ever talk to Jamey any more?"

Stan looked up at her with a mouthful of turkey and dressing.

"Jamey Larson," Dana said, "Remember him?"

"Actually," Stan said, wiping his mouth with his blue linen napkin. "I spoke to Jamey a couple weeks ago."

"So you guys keep in touch? That's great."

"We talk on the phone once in a while."

Dana sat back in the couch, sinking deeper into the cushions. "You two were pretty close back then. It's nice that you keep in touch. I hardly ever talk to anyone from school. It's been so long."

Stan eyed Dana over the rim of his goblet. He took a long thoughtful sip, and set the glass down beside his plate.

"Jamey lives in Miami now. South Beach to be exact. He's in real estate and God knows what else."

"Really? Last I heard he was in Central America, doing a lot of drugs."

Stan shrugged, cutting another bite of turkey. "We all have our skeletons. But he's been through rehab, so now he's drug-free and hawking high-rise buildings and mansions in West Palm Beach."

"So he's okay?" she asked, leaning in closer.

"Hey. He's made millions."

"But how's he doing? Is he married? Any kids?"

Stan laughed, almost choking on his turkey. He took his napkin, wiped his mouth, and then tossed the napkin onto his plate. He leaned back in his chair and pushed his plate away from the edge of the coffee table with his bare foot.

"Jamey is gay, Dana."

Her eyes opened wide. Then she made a conscious effort not to let her mouth gape open as well.

"Oh come on Dana don't look so shocked."

She blinked a few times. "Are you sure?" She finally managed to say.

Stan howled with laughter. Then he reached over and slapped her on the knee. "You're priceless," he said. "Such a comic."

"Well he sure as hell wasn't gay in high school."

Stan glanced at Dana then realized she wasn't kidding. "I believe it was after you two split up, Dana, that he decided to stop hiding it."

"Hiding it?" She laughed. "We were together every single day for over a year. I think I would have noticed if he was gay."

"Dana. I don't want to be rude, but whatever it was you guys did, it was a phase for him. Believe me, the man is definitely a homosexual."

Stunned, Dana sat there staring at Stan. His eyelashes were still just as long and lush as they were when they were kids. She focused on his eyelashes because his words were too much for her to absorb.

"Look," he continued, "I don't know which TV talk show you get your information from, but people don't suddenly wake up as adults and realize they're gay. It's a part of you from a very early age. And it doesn't come and go like a clothing fad."

"So you're saying that whole year Jamey and I were together...all those times we... none of that was real?"

Stan shrugged.

"He took me up to his grandfather's farm. I met his great grandmother. We even picked out names for our kids."

Stan sighed. "I know, Dana. He would've said or done anything he thought you wanted just to keep you happy."

"So all of that was a lie?"

Staring down at his hands, Stan twisted the silver ring on his thumb. "Maybe it wasn't exactly a lie. He needed you. You were his ticket in. His security blanket."

"Oh really?"

"Think about it Dana. Do you have any idea what it was like, growing up gay in Texas back then?" Stan scratched his two-day stubble. "Gay bashing wasn't just politically correct, it was ingrained in you at such an early age that it takes years just to figure out how to deal with it."

Dana stared out the window.

Stan cleared his throat then continued, "But once you finally see the big picture, you think up ways to cope. And being with you was a way for Jamey to cope."

Dana stood up, not quite sure what to say. "I better go."

Stan glanced up at the ceiling then shrugged. "Dana I'm sorry."

Tears welled up in Dana's eyes. So many things flashed through her mind at once: Grandpa Larson's farm in the Texas hill country and his prizewinning hogs. Water skiing with Jamey on Clear Lake. Skipping school and making love for hours on the living room floor at his house while his parents were at work. Dana remembered these things like it was only last year. Why the hell did she still feel seventeen inside even though she was actually twice that age?

Dana wondered how all those memories could be lies. She dreamed about these things occasionally. Jamey's old blue pickup truck. The lizard skin cowboy boots she gave him for his seventeenth birthday. The torn up prom photos he returned to her that awful night when they broke up, dumping them on the driveway at her parents' house along with everything else she'd ever given him.

Dana rubbed her forehead, realizing she had a splitting headache. She looked at Stan and a tear spilled out the corner of her eye. He stood up, two feet in front of her.

He reached for her hand but she jerked it away from him.

"Please don't!" She said this with such acrimony it surprised her.

Equally surprised, Stan backed away slightly.

"You used to call me RAGU. You never really liked me very much did you Stan?"

His eyes narrowed as he watched her try hard not to cry. He paused a moment, then put his hand on her shoulder. "Dana, please don't cry. I can't take responsibility for any more pain. I have enough guilt at the moment, okay?"

She took a deep breath and held it. *He's right. I'm being childish.*

Dana thought of Stan's parents. What are they going through? How does Stan sleep at night? Is he alone, or does he have a companion? Has Stan had to watch a partner die, knowing that his own passing will come soon enough?

She covered her face and turned away. Trying to squelch the tears only seemed to make it worse.

Stan removed his hand from her shoulder.

"I'm so sorry," Dana whispered. "How stupid of me to act like this. You must be going through hell in your life right now."

"Actually," Stan said softly. "I'm just starting to feel at peace."

Dana turned around and looked at him. His blue eyes were always beautiful. But now they seemed even brighter, a truly intense aquamarine. And he actually did seem to radiate peace. He touched her elbow then brushed her hair out of her face.

"Won't you please sit down," he said. "Just for a minute longer."

"Oh, Stan. I hate to impose like this."

"Dana. Life is so short. Just sit down," he grinned at her. "I need to apologize for dubbing you Princess RAGU."

Dana laughed, wiping her face with the back of her hand. Stan sat down on the couch and pointed to the cushion next to him.

"I can't stand it when people leave and they're upset with me," he said. "I never know if I'll see them again."

Dana sat down beside him. He took her hand, pressing it between his thin hands.

"Look at me," he said and waited for Dana to make eye contact then he said, "Dying slow is a blessing in disguise because it teaches you how to live."

Dana looked into his eyes. She hesitated then said, "I wish I could make it all go away somehow."

"Me too," he laughed. He squeezed her hand then released it.

And with that little gesture, that squeeze, Dana felt a sudden jolt of electricity. As if a small piece of Stan's energy was now sinking in beneath her skin. A thousand thoughts raced through her mind all at once. Memories. Emotions. Slivers of their shared childhood. Impossible questions: *How long have you been HIV positive? I had no idea you were gay. Or Jamey either. Did you know about Jamey all along? All through school?*

Stan stared at Dana and she felt the weight of his gaze. How could she formulate her confusion into questions he could possibly answer right now? There was nothing he could say anyway to make all that deception go away.

She glanced at Stan just long enough to see his cheek muscles twitch right before he smiled. Then she stared at the floor. When you get right down to it, why am I here anyway? To make a better impression at work? To get that promotion? To benefit from the suffering of others?

Dana inhaled slowly, and the idea emerged like a sudden puff of wind in a dead calm. She eased into it, watching the wind line across the water, feeling the luff then the lift and the acceleration as the wind filled her sail.

"Would you like to go sailing tomorrow?" she asked.

Stan smiled at her.

"Santa Monica Bay is incredibly beautiful this time of year," she assured him. "And usually the sky is so clear you can see the mountains beyond the downtown city skyline."

"Wow," he said, frowning slightly. He considered it a moment, then relaxed into that same old easy grin she remembered from school.

"Yeah," Stan said, nodding. He looked at her and proffered that heart stopping gorgeous smile. "I'd like that a lot."

"Great. I'll come pick you up at eleven," she said. "Is that okay with you?"

Stan nodded.

They sat on the couch as an awkward silence settled between them like a low-lying fog. Dana glanced around the room as if hoping to find her way out of the self-conscious lull in conversation. Then she saw a framed black and white photograph on the bookshelf of Stan and another guy. They were standing shoulder to shoulder, leaning against a large palm tree in what looked like a tropical resort location.

Dana suddenly turned to Stan and said, "Do you want to bring a friend sailing with us tomorrow? So you won't feel uncomfortable?"

Stan smiled at her.

"I'm just thinking about how you might feel around Brian and me. So please don't hesitate to bring someone else with us if you like."

"Dana. Is that your way of asking if I have a boyfriend?"

She laughed nervously then glanced down at her feet.

Stan patted her knee. "That's him in the photo on the bookshelf. That picture was taken in Cabo San Lucas two years ago."

"Two years ago?"

"Yes," said Stan. "We've been together for three years."

Dana looked up at him and smiled. "That's a long time."

Stan nodded and said, "We met the day I arrived here from Texas. Steven is his name. He's from Big Fork, Montana. He's real small town, just like you and me."

"Where did you meet him?" she asked.

"We met at a party at my agent's house."

Dana said, "Is he an actor?"

Stan laughed, "Who isn't in this town?"

Dana did not laugh. Instead she said, "I'm not. And neither is Brian."

Stan glanced sideways at Dana. "He works for Paramount as a website designer. He's a total computer geek, but I love him."

Dana smiled. "Does he live here with you?"

Stan nodded.

The clock on the mantle struck four and Dana moved to the edge of the couch as if she was ready to get up.

"Steve should be home any time now, if you want to stick around, you can meet him."

"I'd like to Stan, but I really should be going. I still have several meals left to deliver."

Stan reached for her hand and she offered it to him. He squeezed it gently then said, "Fine. We'll be ready when you get here at eleven."

Dana smiled, then reached over and hugged Stan. He tensed up at first then relaxed and hugged her back. "I'm glad our paths crossed again. I'm looking forward to tomorrow."

Dana stood up and fished her car keys out of her pocket. "Me too, Stan."

He held out his hand and Dana shook it. "See you tomorrow at eleven."

"See you then," Dana said and headed outside to her car. As she got in her car she saw Stan wave from the front porch. She waved back and thought of Ernestine and her idea that food should be cooked with love.

Dana delivered the rest of her meals then made her way back home, to the Marina, where she and Brian went for a walk along Venice Beach to watch the sun set over Santa Monica Bay. As Dana walked arm in arm with Brian down the beach, she thought of the photo on Stan's bookcase. She squeezed her husband's hand and sighed, wondering how many more sunsets Stan would see before he died. She hoped that Stan had truly found peace. She wanted to know that kind of peace for herself then wondered if it was only attainable when faced with your own impending death. She watched the sun sink below the horizon and felt lucky to be alive.

Only You

When the eight o'clock bell rang, Laura Gray walked to the head of the class and wrote "MS. GRAY" on the board.

"Good morning," said Laura. "Mrs. Sagefeld is sick today, so I'm your sub."

Several children shifted in their seats, exchanging quick glances.

"After we check roll, we're to work on silent reading until 8:30, then we'll do Chapter 12 in your spelling books."

A little girl in the back row raised her hand. Laura checked the seating chart to find her name.

"Yes, Sadie?"

"Mrs. Sagefeld takes us to the Mac Lab for spelling."

"The Mac Lab?"

"Yes. We type our words three times each, do spell check then retype the ones we missed. After that, we get to play computer games till time for math."

"Oh I see." Thank you Sadie." Laura looked over the lesson plan on her desk and wondered how anyone could expect a sub to figure all that out from the hastily scribbled notes.

After taking a head count for hot lunch requests and checking roll, Laura read over the schedule. Lunch at 11:45 caught her eye. With no time for breakfast this morning, her stomach was already growling.

At 8:30 Laura asked the class to take their spelling books and line up at the door.

"And do it quietly, please," she said.

The students got in line with minimal commotion, except for two little boys. After trading insults and a few shoves, one boy punched the other in the stomach.

"Boys! What's going on here?" Laura demanded, approaching the boys. Neither one spoke. She grabbed them by their wrists. "Do I need to walk you two around like little toddlers? You boys are in third grade now. Let's try to act like well mannered eight-year-olds instead of two-year-olds, shall we?"

The boys glared at one another. When Laura released them, they both got back in line.

"Sadie, will you show me where the Mac Lab is please?"

Sadie nodded and led the class across the open area to the lab, where the children found their seats and quickly turned on their computers. As they began typing their spelling words, Laura was impressed by their computer skills. A sudden crash from behind startled her. She turned to the same two boys fighting again; this time they had shoved a chair against the table.

"Boys! Stop it!"

In a whirl of hitting, kicking and slapping, arms flailed every which way. Laura reached into the fray and grabbed one boy by the back of his collar. She jerked him away from his opponent then snatched the other boy by his belt loop.

"This behavior is entirely unacceptable!"

As she released the smaller boy's belt loop, she noticed his bloody lip. Reaching into her pocket, she pulled out a tissue and gave it to him. He dabbed his lip.

"I want you boys to apologize to everyone in the class," said Laura.

They looked up at her, confused.

"Just say, 'I'm sorry for disturbing you. Please forgive me. I'll never do it again.' And say it like you mean it."

She led the boys around the room and made them apologize to each student individually. She then placed the two boys in the center of the room and asked all the students to turn their chairs around and face them.

Laura stood between the boys. "Now I don't know what usually happens when fighting occurs…"

Sadie raised her hand and blurted out, "They have to go to the principal's office."

Ignoring Sadie, Laura continued, "But today we're going to share a little story about the interconnectedness of the universe."

Confused, the children stared at Laura. Some giggled.

"You've never heard of this before?"

They shook their heads collectively.

"It means that everything you do affects everything else. Whether it's lying, stealing, or hugging a friend, it affects us all because we are all connected."

Sitting down on the floor, Laura made the two boys sit beside her then motioned for all the other children to join them.
"Come sit here with us for story time."

The children snickered a little, but complied. When they all settled down, Laura began her story.

"Okay. Suppose you're walking home from school one day and you pass an elderly gentleman sitting on the sidewalk with his face in his hands. He's crying. So you ask him if he's okay.

"He immediately takes a swing at you and yells at you to leave him alone. You feel sorry for the old man, so once again you ask if he needs help. This time he calls you a nasty name and tries to hit you with his cane. What would you do now?"

Laura waited for a response. Silence hung on the air like wet laundry.

"Kick him in the shins for calling you a nasty name?" Laura asked. "No? Would you leave him there or try and help him?"

A freckle-faced girl with pigtails raised her hand. Laura pointed at her.

"I'd call the police."

"Why?" Laura asked. "What would they do?"

"Put him in jail."

Laura stifled a laugh. "Okay, let's try this again. Suppose the man has blood on his hands and knees; obviously he's fallen. Would this make a difference in how you treat him?"

Laura reached over and tapped the shoulder of the boy beside her. Glancing up at her, he licked the cut on his lip.

"What about you, Tommy? How would you treat this man after he called you names and tried to whack you with his cane?"

Tommy glared at his opponent seated beside Laura then crossed his arms over his chest. "People who try to hit you for no reason are losers so I'd leave the old fart right where he was."

As the class erupted in laughter, the other boy leaned over towards Tommy, behind Laura's back.

"You started it, you little prick!" He shoved Tommy again.

Laura intervened, separating the two boys.

"Name callers are pretty worthless too," Tommy retorted.

"Boys!" Laura slapped her thighs in frustration. "It's exactly this kind of behavior I'm talking about."

A Long haired boy on the back row raised his hand. Laura pointed to him and the boy said, "So what does this old geezer on the sidewalk have to do with anything?"

Laura sighed. "It's supposed to illustrate how we make choices every day. Choices that only we can make. And that these choices have consequences. For instance, suppose the old man on the sidewalk was being harassed by a group of kids. Suppose they even threw rocks at him. What would you do?"

Sadie raised her hand. Laura nodded at her.

"I'd tell them to stop since he probably got lost from the nursing home and needed his pills."

Laura hesitated then nodded slowly. "That's interesting. Sadie brings up a very good point here. Because there's probably a logical explanation for the old man's behavior. Even though it may seem strange to us. Maybe he has Alzheimer's and needs medication to keep him from being confused.

"At any rate, suppose you do as Sadie suggests and try to make the other kids leave him alone. But they laugh at you and start calling you names. You try to explain that the old man obviously needs help, but they don't listen. Instead, they throw rocks at you. So now you have to decide whether to go along with the crowd and torment the old man too, or go home and pretend you never saw it. But what about this: would anyone think to call 911 for help?"

Laura folded her arms, studying her student's faces.

"Which one of these options would you choose?"

No one responded so Laura prodded them a little.

"Don't you see? We're all faced with choices like this every day. You can choose to take a risk and help someone else, even though they've called you names and taken a swing at you, or you can ignore it and do nothing, thinking it's not your problem. Or you could simply get angry and try to hit them back. Either way, it's a choice that only you can make."

The long haired boy in the back row raised his hand again. "Yeah but these two dweebs always fight. So what's that got to do with the old guy in the story?"

"Okay," Laura said. "Let's suppose that because the old man tried to hit you with his cane that you decide to go home and leave him there. It's none of your business, right? So you take your time, stopping at the park to play baseball with your friends. And you forget all about the old man.

"But when you get home, your mom runs out of the house, very upset, and tells you to get in the car. She drives really fast to the hospital, and on the way she explains that something has happened to your grandfather. Now you remember the old man on the sidewalk and you regret your decision not to get involved.

"All the way to the hospital, you have a sinking feeling that you should have helped that old man. When you finally get there, you find your grandmother in the waiting room, crying."

Several of the students started to fidget. Laura hesitated, wondering if the story was making sense to them. Then she continued.

"Your mom finally explains that your grandfather was attacked and beaten by some gang kids earlier that afternoon. You cringe, thinking of the old man on the sidewalk. But as it turns out, your grandpa was attacked at a convenience store way across town. Fortunately, someone witnessed the attack and called 911. He was hurt pretty bad, but survived because someone took action. This is the point of the story: someone made a choice to help your grandfather and because of that choice, he is still alive."

Laura leaned in toward her class, holding out her hands, palms up. "Do you get it now?" She glanced at her student's faces, sensing they were actually beginning to understand.

"You see? We all have ONLY YOU situations every day. They may not always be life threatening, like the one with your grandfather. In fact, they might be as silly as being called a nasty name by a stranger, or even a classmate. At any rate, only you can choose how you'll react. And it's your reaction that often has the most impact on the entire situation."

Laura paused. The students stared at her, expectant; a hush settled over the room like fog rolling in off the bay.

"So I want all of you to remember this, the next time anyone calls you a name, or treats you unfairly. Think about how you can turn it into an ONLY YOU situation."

The long haired boy in the back row raised his hand again then he stood up and said, "It's past time to start on our math."

"Oh," said Laura, glancing at her watch. "You're right."

She led the students back to their classroom and instructed them to get out their measuring tapes. While passing out worksheets, Laura told them to choose a partner and work together to make sure they understood the assignment. Then she read the following questions from the worksheet.

"What is the length of your arm-span? What is the circumference of your wrist? What is the width of your foot?"

After explaining the definition of arm-span, circumference and width, Laura told the children to help each other use their measuring tapes to find the lengths for all their questions.

As the students worked busily measuring themselves and each other, Laura noticed that they were talking a little too loudly. "Class!" Laura shouted, trying to make herself heard. "We need to talk softly so we don't disturb the other classes."

Just as Laura spoke, a teacher from a classroom across the open area came stomping up to Laura's classroom and scolded the children.

"You students are entirely too loud! I've been watching and I've taken note of who's out of their chair. You need to respect your neighbors, or I'll have to report you."

Laura stared at the woman, shocked that any teacher would so brazenly intrude on another class like that, and embarrassed that her students had been loud enough to disturb another class clear across the open area. When the teacher left, Laura told her students to finish their math worksheets tomorrow. Then she asked them to get out their social studies books, read chapter six silently and complete the chapter review on their own.

"There's to be no talking. And no getting up from your chair. If you have a question, raise your hand and I'll come answer you."

As Laura walked between the rows of desks, helping the students who raised their hands, she had an eerie feeling that the teacher across the way was watching her. Glancing up periodically, she actually caught the disagreeable woman staring at her more than once. Each time, Laura turned her back and continued answering questions.

At lunch time, Laura escorted her students to the cafeteria and told them she would return in thirty minutes to take them back to class. She stood in line and bought a grilled cheese sandwich and a pint of orange juice then went to the teachers' lounge to eat.

As soon as she entered the room, several teachers looked up at her then stared back down at their food. A hush fell like a sudden spring rain. As Laura found a seat, she noticed the teacher who reprimanded her class was sitting at the far end of the table. Feeling awkward, Laura tried to break the silence.

"Hi. I'm Laura Gray. Nice to meet you all."

No one spoke. Laura peeled open her orange juice carton.

"I apologize if my class disturbed any of you in the open area. I'm afraid they were a little boisterous earlier."

"I'm Harriet Westerly and I accept your apology, since your class definitely disturbed mine."

Laura stared at the woman then forced a smile. Unfolding the paper wrapper from her sandwich, she wondered why anyone would be so intentionally rude.

"Is this your first time to sub?" asked Harriet.

"No," Laura said, shifting in her chair. I'm new to this district, but I've been subbing for years."

"Oh really? Well, since you couldn't control your class, I thought maybe it was your first time."

No longer hungry, Laura put her sandwich down. She took a deep breath, cleared her throat and said, "Actually, Mrs. Westerly, I had complete control of my class. Their assignment was to measure specific body lengths, working with partners, using their tape measures, and that's exactly what they did."

"Relax, honey. You don't need to make excuses, we've all been there. These kids will run all over you if you let them."

A young teacher stood up from the table, threw away her trash and then left the lounge. Laura stared at her uneaten sandwich and thought about her ONLY YOU story. She felt like a hypocrite. How could she teach these children to turn the other cheek then be unable to do it herself?

Another teacher, a perky brunette, cleared her throat and said, "So is anyone going to Sharon's Tupperware party?"

An in depth discussion ensued, on the latest innovation in plastic food storage containers. Laura grabbed her uneaten sandwich, dumped it in the trash and left the lounge.s

Trembling with anger, Laura hurried down the hall to the restroom. She washed her hands then said under her breath, "The nerve of that bitch." She got out her lipstick and leaned over the sink towards the mirror. A toilet flushed then the young teacher who'd gotten up and left the lounge came out from the stall and washed her hands at the sink next to Laura.

She glanced over at Laura and said, "Listen. Don't pay any attention to Harriet. She loves to stir up trouble. No one takes her seriously around here, so you shouldn't either."

Laura smiled. "Thanks." She finished applying her lipstick then blotted it with a tissue. "You know," said Laura, "I don't think I've ever met such a confrontational person in my entire life."

The other teacher laughed. "I thought the exact same thing when I first met her last year. But don't let her get to you. She's really got a good heart, deep down." She smiled warmly then held out her hand. "Alice Wilson, nice to meet you."

They shook hands.

"Laura Gray. Thanks for the advice."

"No problem."

After the final bell rang, and the last child left the room, Laura straightened the piles of completed assignments and stacked them beside the lesson plan.

Exhausted, she massaged her temples, trying to alleviate her splitting headache. She grabbed her bag and hurried out of the open area, then realized she had left her sunglasses. She returned to the classroom, found her sunglasses in the top desk drawer then stuck them in her pocket. Recalling her run-in with Harriet, she hesitated then glanced across the open area. There was Harriet, sitting hunched like a gargoyle at her desk, grading papers.

Considering Alice's opinion that Harriet was basically a good person deep down, Laura watched her a moment, then wondered what could make a person behave in such a negative manner. She felt sorry for Harriet, then instantly felt compelled to talk to her once more.

Laura walked into the open space between the classroom modules then stopped. "Wait a minute," she said to herself. "Harriet will respond exactly like she did this morning." Laura turned abruptly and headed back towards the exit.

As the passed the Mac Lab, she remembered her ONLY YOU story. If she left without speaking to Harriet, wouldn't she be just like the child who left the old man on the sidewalk? Harriet's knees might not be bloody at the moment, but she definitely exhibited symptoms of being in pain.

Laura drew herself up, ready for whatever might happen next. She turned and marched straight back to Harriet's classroom and stood before her desk. Harriet looked up then lowered her glasses so she could see over them.

"Yes?" asked Harriet.

"Mrs. Westerly, I just wanted you to know that I'm sorry if I offended you. Also, I can't help wondering if you might have some sort of burden making you unhappy, or what I meant is, perhaps there's something I can do to help you."

Harriet frowned. "What exactly do you mean by that?"

"I just thought a little kindness might go a long way."

Harriet laughed. She took off her glasses and laid them on her desk. "I see you're not only incompetent as a teacher, but as a humanitarian as well."

Laura stiffened.

"Don't look so surprised. Did you really think I would lie down on a couch and tell you my life story? I mean come on. Let's drop this little holier than thou façade, shall we?"

Laura sighed and shook her head slowly. "I don't know why I bothered. Never mind." She turned and walked away, Harriet's words burning in her ears. Once again, she allowed this unpleasant woman to upset her; and even with noble intentions, Laura still managed to offend Harriet. "Maybe she's right," she said to herself. "Maybe I am incompetent."

Laura hurried across the parking lot to her car. She felt ridiculous and empty. Her head pounded. She needed something sweet, so she decided to stop at Dairy Queen on the way home and treat herself to an Oreo Cookie Blizzard.

After leaving the Dairy Queen, Laura drove to the city park and sat at a picnic bench watching the ducks on the pond and savoring her Oreo Cookie Blizzard. She tried to relax, and put the day's events behind her. After thirty minutes, it started raining so she got back in her car and began the long trek home.

Even in her rural school district, Laura's home was well off the beaten path. She lived way out on the west shore of Cedar Lake. It usually took at least thirty minutes to drive out from town, but today with the rain, it took even longer.

Just as Laura rounded a sharp curve in the road, she saw a deer dart out into the street up ahead. Laura braked, and waited for the deer to move; but it just stood there, frozen in the middle of the street. Another deer ran out into the road with a fawn behind it. The deer sniffed and nuzzled each other.

Suddenly a Ford Bronco rounder the sharp curve up ahead. Seeing the deer in the road, the driver slammed on the brakes and immediately skidded out of control. The deer leapt back into the safety of the trees, but the Bronco spun around twice then slammed into the wooden guard rail on the side of the road. It crashed through the rail, careening down the steep embankment into Cedar Creek about thirty feet below the road.

Laura pulled off the road, dialed 911 on her cell phone and reported the accident, then jumped out of her car and made her way down through the brush to the wreckage. Half immersed in the creek, the Bronco laid on its side, with smoke pouring out from the grill. Laura ran up to the vehicle and peeked through the smashed windshield.

Horrified, she recoiled and tried to collect herself. The woman behind the wheel was unconscious and blood oozed from a huge gash across her face. Laura pulled off her jacket and wrapped it around her fist. There was an opening in the cracked glass just large enough for her hand so she reached in and pressed her jacket against the woman's head, trying to stop the bleeding. When she heard a child crying from the back seat, she panicked. She jumped, ripping her sleeve against a shard. After carefully extricating her arm from between the pieces of shattered glass, she ran around the Bronco and tried to look inside. But a large tree lay jammed up against the driver side door, preventing her access. The passenger side door was under water. So Laura kicked in the shattered back window and crawled in over the tailgate. Peering over the back seat, Laura saw a young girl pinned up against the passenger side door.

"Are you hurt honey," Laura said.

The little girl whimpered softly.

"Can you move?"

The girl nodded and pushed the wooden crate off her.

"Great!" said Laura. "Can you crawl over here towards me?"

The girl inched slowly towards Laura and reached out her tiny hand. She trembled as Laura grabbed her and pulled her up out of the creek water which was slowly seeping into the vehicle. With all the strength she could muster, Laura hoisted the child up over the back seat then cradled her in her arms.

When the girl began to shiver uncontrollably, Laura knew she didn't have much time; the child was apparently going into shock. She climbed out of the wreckage and carried the child up the muddy creek bank, struggling through the thick underbrush and back up the steep embankment. When she finally reached her car, she started the engine and turned on the heater. She wrapped the girl in a coffee stained bedspread which she'd thrown into her trunk last week and still hadn't found the time to drop off at the dry cleaners.

"Can you hear me?" Laura asked the girl.

The child nodded slightly, still shivering. She suddenly opened her eyes and said, "My mommy's having a baby."

Laura blinked. The woman behind the wheel. Oh my god, she's pregnant. "Stay here honey; don't get out of the car."

Laura left the child and hurried back down to the wreckage. When she reached the woman, she found her slumped down in the seat, leaning way over towards the passenger side, which was filling up with dark creek water. The woman's neck and shoulders were partially submerged, with water just inches away from her face.

Laura took off her boots, but them on her hands like boxing gloves and began pounding her fists at the windshield. Finally she was able to clear away enough of the shattered glass so that she could lean inside and lift the woman's head up out of the water. She felt the woman's neck for a pulse.

Finding nothing at first, Laura kept trying until she thought she felt a faint pulse beneath her fingertips.

"Hang on!" Laura whispered. "Help is on the way."

Unresponsive, the woman hung limp in Laura's hands. Worried that she'd been feeling her own pulse in her fingertips rather than the woman's pulse, she lifted the woman's eyelids. Her eyes rolled up in her head, with only the whites showing.

Laura panicked. "Your daughter is in my car, warm and safe. Any minute now, they'll be here to get you out. Just hang on."

As the rainstorm worsened, the creek water inched higher and higher lapping at the Bronco. When the paramedics finally arrived on the scene, Laura stood waist-deep in the rushing creek, trying desperately to keep the woman's head above water.

Within minutes, the rescue team cut the woman out of the vehicle then loaded her and her daughter into the County General ambulance. Then the rain suddenly stopped.

Standing by the roadside, soaking wet, Laura watched the ambulance pull away, lights flashing, and for some odd reason she thought of Harriet Westerly. Immediately she laughed aloud. A policeman standing beside her filling out his report asked if she was okay.

"Yes I'm fine," said Laura. She pulled her jacket up closer around her shoulder. "I just realized the only reason I came along when I did was because of a confrontation I had at work today. It was so upsetting that I went to the park for a half hour and tried to calm down, instead of driving straight home after work."

The cop pushed his cap back and scratched his forehead.

"You know, if not for that confrontation, I would have already been home when they crashed. There's no telling how long they would have been down in that creek before someone else came by and saw them way down there."

Laura looked up at the policeman.

"Yeah," he nodded. "Not much traffic out here is there?"

Laura smiled. "That's the beauty of living out this far. But believe it or not, I was driving along trying not to think about what a bitch this lady had been to me today, then this happened. And now I realize that her bitchiness is probably what saved their lives, since it's precisely what delayed me."

The policeman chuckled. He flipped the page on his clipboard and said, "Well that's one way to look at it."

Laura smiled. She wiped her wet hair from her face then glanced up at the sky. The storm had passed, and she could just make out the faintest trace of a rainbow as the sun sank between billowy gray curtains of clouds.

Recovering Sky

Lying flat on her back on the living room floor, Sherry Davis squeezed her eyes shut and pretended she finally looked slim and toned like the fitness instructor in her exercise DVD. When the phone rang she opened her eyes and felt the sting of sweat as it blurred her vision. Reaching to the coffee table for the remote, she paused the DVD then pulled herself up and ran into the kitchen to answer the phone.

It was Beth, the woman whose name was just above Sherry's on their church prayer chain phone list.

"Bad news today, Sherry." Beth was talking fast, upset by the message she had to relay. "A twelve-year-old girl is missing. She went out riding her bike this morning and never came back."

"Oh no," Sherry whispered. She grabbed her notebook, flipped to a clean page and started writing. A drop of sweat fell from her chin, bleeding the ink on the word missing.

"She left early this morning, around seven o'clock. Her parents said she'd never take off like this and not tell them where she was going, especially on a school day."

"What's her name?" Sherry asked.

"Sky Jacobi."

Closing her notebook, Sherry glanced at the clock. The girl had been gone roughly eight hours. Anything could have happened by now.

"One more thing," Beth said. "They've asked for volunteers to walk the rice fields out there along the bayou."

"Okay. I'll pass the word along."

As she hung up the phone, Sherry tried to imagine what this little girl looked like. Skinny? Knobby-kneed? Pigtails? She felt an odd shudder across her shoulder blades and the back of her neck. She grabbed her phone list and dialed the next number.

The following day was Good Friday. Sherry got up early so she could drive her mother to church. Dozens of people greeted her mother, saying things like, "You look so good!" or "It's great to see you out and about!" Or "What a perfect hat!"

Sherry smiled, watching as her mom's eyes literally sparkled. Clearly these people adored her mother. Some of them even told her they were praying for her. Her mother thanked them all, obviously moved by their encouragement. Sherry turned away, unable to watch any longer. In truth, her mother was extremely tired. Dark circles sagged under her eyes. Her skin looked almost yellow today. What was left of her hair had started falling out again. This was the tenth month of her chemotherapy.

To say Sherry felt confident about her mother's chances of recovery would have been a lie. This type of cancer was quite rare, with less than a two percent survival rate. But her mother refused to relegate herself to medical jargon and statistics. She chose faith instead. Turning back to watch as her mother's friends congregated around her, Sherry felt heartened by their compassion but recognized a burgeoning darkness inside herself.

She was angry and afraid, but she never let her mother see this. A virtual hurricane brewed beneath her calm façade of self-control.

Sherry glanced at her mother's hands cupped absently against her thighs. They seemed so frail, so ancient and foreign; her veins protruding like little blue ribbons rippling against faded parchment. Those hands had wiped away her tears, braided her hair, and pressed her forehead to feel for fever. Those hands had taught her to sew. To write. To pray. An eternity of love rested in those gentle palms. Sherry couldn't imagine a world where those hands no longer existed.

While her mother visited with friends in the foyer, Sherry ducked into the tiny prayer chapel adjacent to the sanctuary. A dozen candles burned on the altar beside a photograph of a young girl. Sherry stared at the photo, realizing it was Sky. She had braces and braids. Sherry wondered if Sky was frightened or in pain right now. Approaching the altar, she took a deep breath and touched the photo; immediately the dam cracked under pressure. Clutching the frame to her chest, Sherry hung her head, sobbing.

During the service, the minister spoke of Sky's disappearance, thanking those who had helped in the search and requesting more volunteers. Sherry considered volunteering, but decided against it since she had to work that afternoon. After teaching two aerobics classes, then covering the front desk till the gym closed, Sherry knew she'd be exhausted. Maybe next week she told herself then cringed at the thought of Sky being missing for that long.

Driving home, Sherry noticed her mom dozing in the passenger seat so she turned off the radio. Biting her lip, she glanced over at her mother. Several strands of hair had fallen onto her mother's shoulder. Sherry reached up and plucked them from her mother's blouse.

Sherry's husband Jay played sax in a local blues band and tonight they were performing at a bar on Egret Bay called the Cross Eyed Seagull. Sherry showered at the gym then raced to the club, but the second set had already started by the time she arrived. She found an empty stool at the bar and ordered a beer. The place felt like a sauna with moist, sweaty bodies compressed into a small space.

After the final set, Sherry sat with her husband and the rest of the band while they finished their beers and waited for the manager to pay them. At 2 a.m. she told Jay she wanted to go home. He asked her to wait for him to load out the gear so she wouldn't have to drive home alone, but she assured him she was okay to drive. Besides, she knew how long 'loading out' usually took; then the guys in the band would want to eat breakfast at the IHOP. It would definitely be after four by the time Jay got home.

A few hours later, Jay crawled into bed smelling like bacon and cigarettes. Sherry rolled over towards him but he began snoring immediately. She sighed. It was nearly dawn now and she still couldn't fall asleep. She rolled back onto her side and put a pillow over her head hoping to muffle the sound of Jay's snores. It didn't help. She stared out from under the pillow, watching the night give way to dawn as a pale light crept through the mini blinds and threw fragmented shadows across the bedroom wall. Wide awake, she decided to get up and watch the early morning news.

The search for Sky dominated the local networks. During an interview with Sky's family, her mother said in a shaky voice, "I feel in my heart that Sky is still out there somewhere, being protected by her own special angels. And I'd just like to say to whoever has her that it's time to bring her home." Then she broke down sobbing.

Hot tears streamed down Sherry's cheeks. She switched off the TV and stared out of the window. Streaks of orange and pink light dissected the sky. She turned off the lamp so she could sit in darkness and watch the beauty of this sunrise from the window bench. Tomorrow is Easter Sunday, Sherry told herself. At church they would celebrate life conquering death. But coping with her mother's illness and now the search for this missing child had all but robbed Sherry of the joy she usually felt during Easter.

"Get a grip," she said to herself. "And stop being so damn morbid."

She got up and made a cup of herbal tea. And as she sat there dunking her tea bag, she came to a stark realization. It wasn't the inevitability of death that bothered her; it was the uncertainty of life. It was the chaos. The mystery. All those tiny details which somehow added up to equal a life worth living. How many more sunrises to be witnessed? How many hugs? How much time was left to do and see and become all we possibly can in this life?

In the back of her mind loomed the fear that her mother wouldn't see another Easter. Though she knew she should be thankful for whatever time her mother had left, Sherry couldn't help feeling cheated. Sitting there alone in the dark, she felt dwarfed by the enormity of death. Death was so much bigger than any one single life. She felt tiny. Depressed. Restless.

"This is ridiculous," she said to her teacup. She put the cup down, took off her robe and started her exercise DVD. But before she could even break a sweat, she felt so incredibly anxious she had to turn it off. She sat down on the living room floor and cried.

After her tears subsided, the urge to get out of the house and do something constructive beset her. She dressed quickly, in a pair of jeans and a sweatshirt, and decided to drive to Home Depot to look for wisteria trees for an Easter present for her parents. Sherry had dug out a flowerbed in the back yard last summer when she and Jay first returned home to help care for her mom during her illness. There was a wooden swing in the center of the flowerbed and Sherry was planning to plant roses and lilies around the pine trees to create a quiet little spot where her mom could go and relax in a garden of her own. Her mother loved the way wisteria smelled when it bloomed, and she especially loved the velvety soft petals that carpeted the ground beneath the trees.

Sherry grabbed her purse and hurried outside, surprised that the air was still chilly enough to see her breath fog. Although it wasn't quite seven o'clock, it was so gray outside that it felt more like dusk than daybreak. But as she backed her car down the long driveway, her mood lightened and she thought of her hands in the loamy soil creating something alive for her mother.

On her way back home, as she drove over the Coward's Creek Bridge with two small wisteria trees tucked into her hatchback, Sherry noticed several people down by the creek bank. She counted at least five men in the tall grass, maybe more. They wore army fatigues and knee high rubber boots, and carried long wooden sticks. And they each had a loop of yellow ribbon pinned to their shirts. Their tenacity amazed her. It was early Saturday morning and they were already out searching for Sky. Feeling compelled to help search, Sherry quickly unloaded the wisteria trees and carried them to the back yard, then hurried back across the street to join the searchers. She waved at the man lagging behind.

"Hi. Mind if I join you?"

He stared at her, confused.

"I live across the street," she explained pointing over her shoulder. "I grew up here, so I know these trails pretty well."

He scratched his beard. "Well, you're supposed to sign up at headquarters. They've got to be able to account for everyone, so no one else turns up missing."

"Fair enough."

"But…" he hesitated, thinking aloud. "I have my cell phone with me. I suppose we could call in and add your name to our list."

"Great. I'm Sherry Davis."

"Hal Lester." He shook her hand. "Right now we're mainly looking for anything hidden from aerial view. Whatever the search planes may've missed. Check inside any culverts or suspicious looking plastic garbage bags. Stuff like that."

"Okay. Got it." She glanced downstream at the others, glad to be a part of their group. "By the way, I left my cell phone at home. Should I go get it?"

"Sure. Good idea. Then if we get separated, you can call in if you find anything or need help."

Sherry climbed back up the embankment and ran home to get the phone. Pulling it out of her bag, she discovered the dead battery. It only required twenty minutes to recharge, so she plugged it in. She went outside to the garage and searched through her father's shelves of fishing gear for his waders. Finding them at last, she pulled them on even though they were of course way too big for her.

Half an hour later, she returned to the creek but the search team was gone. She stuffed the phone into her shirt pocket and buttoned the flap. Standing there, jamming her stick down into the soggy bank, she watched a plastic water bottle float downstream. She didn't want to go home so she decided to search on her own. What could it hurt? She knew these trails like the back of her hand.

Following the path down to Yancey's pond, she realized what should have been obvious to her all along. It had been about twenty years since she'd seen these trails. The city Drainage District had recently built a new pump station making it impossible to reach the pond from the old trail. A posh new neighborhood now obliterated the bulk of the old trails around the pond. A row of houses backed up to the creek, each yard separated by its own ten-foot fence. Thomas Wolfe was right; you can't go home again.

Sherry decided to wade across the creek and approach the park from the north. Fetid brown water sloshed up against her, spilling over her dad's waders, soaking her clothes. She knew this place was a breeding ground for poisonous snakes such as water moccasins and cottonmouths, but she pushed the thought from her mind. Reaching the north side of the creek, she scrambled up the bank and checked the cell phone-- still dry. She pulled off her dad's boots and dumped out all the water. The caked mud smelled like manure.

A mosquito bit her on the neck. She slapped it then looked at her hand. A bloody pulp of insect remains rested on her palm. Wiping it on the sleeve of her denim shirt, she wondered if that blood belonged to her or an earlier donor.

After walking a mile or so down the trail, she spotted a black plastic garbage bag. She poked her stick at it. It was full. And it stunk. Her heart pounded. She jabbed it again and this time it felt like a mound of flesh. She held her breath and ripped open the bag. It was full of garbage and a dead rat crawling with maggots.

Recoiling, she turned away and nearly vomited, the stench was so strong. As she ran down the trail to escape the odor, she remembered running these trails as a child. She could see herself as a ten-year-old tomboy racing down the trail, dodging low hanging vines and moss covered branches as her kid brother ran ahead of her, disappearing into the trees up ahead.

Still running, she tripped over a thorny vine and stumbled into a poison ivy patch. She fell to her knees, catching herself with her stick, then stood up slowly, scratching the mosquito bites on the back of her neck. Another one bit her on the hand. She slapped it away. The thorns left a grid of small scratches down her forearms. She watched tiny drops of blood surface in one of the deeper cuts.

Sherry wondered how many other men and women just like her were stomping through fields and muddy creek beds right now. Last night on the news, it was reported that more than two thousand people were helping in the Sky recovery effort. Surely with all these volunteers, somebody will find her.

Reaching a fork in the trail, Sherry chose the path that led away from the creek. The brush was densely overgrown. The trail almost completely disappeared: it was mangled with vines, underbrush and thick clumps of bamboo. Her arms burned as sweat seeped into her cuts and scratches.

She could hear the search helicopters circling overhead. This felt as futile as war. These trails were not at all like the secret garden she remembered from childhood. More like a steamy jungle. The trees formed an arc overhead so thick and lush their leaves almost blocked out the sky. This dark space beneath the trees felt like a crypt. When the helicopters finally passed, the cries of frogs and birds and locusts emerged then crescendoed into a full-scale anthem. Standing still, she gazed up at the scattered patches of blue peeking through the canopy of trees and sagging Spanish moss. Right then, the sky's cool ambivalence offered little hope of recovering Sky.

Half a mile further down, she reached the creek again, approaching the backside of the Old City Park. She climbed down the steep embankment as cautiously as she could, and then lost her footing just as she reached the water. Flat on her back in the mire, Sherry jumped as a large turtle splashed beside her then disappeared beneath the surface. Mud splattered across her neck and shoulders. Stringy with muck, her hay colored hair smelled disgusting. She was filthy. "Why the hell am I doing this?" she asked herself then used her stick to pull herself back up.

She glanced up and down the creek, terrified of snakes. Again she banished the thought and started back across the creek. Fortunately, the water here was only knee deep. When she finally reached mid-stream, her stick hit something ominous on the creek bed in front of her. It felt exactly like that trash bag she had stumbled upon earlier. Afraid of finding another maggoty rat, she hurried toward the shore.

Safely on the other side, she gazed back at the water. Dozens of honeysuckle blossoms floated on the surface. More than a week had passed since the last rain so there was hardly any current. Thus, the strange little ripple in mid-stream puzzled her. There were no signs of submerged rocks or tree trunks, nothing to make the water swirl around like that. So what had she hit with her stick? She took a deep breath, thankful it smelled like honeysuckle here instead of a pigsty.

Reluctantly, she stepped back in the water, probing with her stick in front of her, feeling nothing but a muddy creek bed until reaching the center. She paused a moment then pushed her stick down into the water. It hit something firm. Dense. Moving her left foot slowly toward her stick, she felt something hard and heavy against her dad's rubber boot. She stepped back; pulse racing. She reached for her cell phone then hesitated. What would she say?

"Hi. I found something hard and firm in the creek but couldn't pull it up to look at it yet because I'm afraid of maggoty rats."

Trying to remain calm, she continued probing around with her stick until she hit something again. She reached down into the cool dark water, which came up past her elbow, almost to her shoulder. Finding a large rock, she tried to pick it up but couldn't. Something was tied to it. It felt like a cord. Frightened of what she'd find, she dropped it, took a few deep breaths, and then froze. Something red, barely visible, appeared just below the murky surface.

It looked like a rag. She jabbed her stick into it and tried to pull it up out of the muddy water. It was heavy but she kept pulling. It must have weighed eighty or ninety pounds. She managed to lift it up a few inches until she could see a red T-shirt looped round with cord; the same cord tied to the rock.

Her hands trembled as she reached down and grabbed the shirt. She pulled it up and stringy blond hair emerged from beneath the water. Sherry turned the body over, finding a bloated face with blue skin, the mouth gagged with a bandana and a red sock. Panicking, Sherry dropped the body right there. Her ears rang. She felt nauseous.

She sloshed back to the bank, grabbed a large tree root and pulled herself up the muddy slope. She leaned against the tree, breathing hard. Her mouth watered and her hands shook violently as she dialed 911 on her cell phone. She closed her eyes but still saw that blond head, face down in the creek. Then she vomited.

According to the FBI, the blond girl recovered from the creek was named Sarah, not Sky. She would have been eleven next month. Abducted from Galveston two weeks ago, she was now going home but not the way her family had hoped. In the newspaper, Sherry read that Sarah's family mourned her death but were grateful that their frantic search was finally over.

Several weeks later, Sherry received a letter from Sarah's mother, thanking her for finding her daughter and answering her prayers. In her letter, Sarah's mother called Sherry an angel for going out alone to search for a child she didn't even know.

Sherry kept the letter on the bookshelf beside her bed. She had trouble sleeping at night, so she developed the habit of reading something pleasant just before turning off the light. Tonight she'd read the same page of "Lord of the Rings" several times and still had no idea what it said. Jay glanced at her book, then at the clock.

"At this rate you'll be sixty before you finish this book," he said.

Sherry looked over at him. He smiled then took the book out of her hands. He dog-eared the page and put it on the shelf then reached for the letter from Sarah's mother. He read it aloud to Sherry. Slow. Methodical. Tracing his fingers against the back of her hand as he spoke.

"I'm hardly an angel," Sherry interrupted.

"This woman seems to disagree with you." Jay folded the letter and placed it back in its envelope. "You still dozing off at work in the afternoons?

Sherry nodded. "I wish I could sleep at night."

"So do I." Jay reached across Sherry's side of the bed and turned off the lamp. "You gotta relax," he said, rubbing her shoulder. "Give it some time."

"You're right," she said. "But I'd rather be giving time to something else far more precious like my mother and her recovery." Sherry yawned and stared at the ceiling. After a few moments she leaned up on one elbow and gazed at Jay in the dark.

"What is it?" he asked yawning.

She shook her head and rolled over facing the wall. He stroked her hair. "Take one of your pills," he said.

"No. They make me crazy."

"And this is sane? Come on babe, you've got to get over this."

In three minutes his breathing hit that steady rhythm of untroubled sleep. Sherry wanted to scream. Running her fingers repeatedly through her hair, she told herself that this would pass with time. She inhaled deep and held her breath. Life goes on, with or without our consent. Guaranteeing nothing except the endless ebb and flow, the constant giving and taking away of itself.

Turning to face Jay as he slept, she slowed her breathing to match his. She tried to imagine what their lives would be like when this insanity was finally over. Sure circumstances change, she reassured herself, but in one way or another, weren't we all simply racing down our own unique trails together?

Two weeks later, Sherry asked Jay to walk with her down those childhood trails. He took her hand as they descended the embankment to Coward's Creek. Pushing low branches out of the way, he stepped aside to let her pass. Standing more than a foot taller than her, Jay had to duck beneath the thick moss. He reached up and yanked a clump down from the branch overhead and held it out to her.

"Gross!" She pushed his hand away.

He laughed. "Centuries ago the French Creoles in Louisiana named this stuff Spanish moss." He tossed it down in the grass. "And then the Spanish promptly dubbed it French hair."

Sherry giggled nervously. Sensing her apprehension, Jay told her several of his best jokes. Though she had heard them all before, she laughed at each one, mainly to keep those images of Sarah at bay.

"We need music," he said, then whistled the Three Stooges theme song. When he started whistling "Love Me Do," Sherry joined him because whistling made her feel better. Lighter. Comforted amid chaos. As they segued into "I Want to Hold Your Hand," they followed the trail from the creek into a clearing. When they stepped out of the dense woods, leaving the canopy of trees behind, it was as if the sky opened above them. And it was then that Sherry realized she was no longer afraid.

She took a deep breath then wrapped her arms around Jay, hugging him.

"What is it?" he asked.

"Thank you," she said. "Thank you for coming here with me."

Jay had given her this gift, a simple reassurance in the midst of tragedy— the proverbial ebb and flow—the give and take of life and death. And with this realization, Sherry took comfort in the immensity of life all around her.

She stood perfectly still then gazed up at the blue sky overhead, feeling safe in Jay's presence beneath their own private swatch of this vast recovering sky.

Melissa L. White

Business News

"Business news," said Veronica D'Angelo, answering the phone on the first ring. She held the phone between her left ear and her shoulder and continued to type at her computer.

"I'm sorry," said Veronica glancing across the newsroom. "Mr. Tinkham is on another line right now. Would you like to hold or should I take a message?"

Veronica stopped typing.

"No, the editor is away from his desk," she said. "Would you like to leave a message for him instead?" She grabbed her message pad and scribbled the tirade of words spewing from the receiver into her ear.

Veronica hung up the phone and took the message to the Business editor's office, placing it directly on top of his phone. He couldn't miss it.

Returning to her desk, she passed by Greg Tinkham, the banking and finance reporter. Greg waved at Veronica from his desk then continued his performance with his phone pressed to his ear. It amazed Veronica how this man would gesture and point and shake his fist at whomever he happened to be speaking to on the phone, as if they could actually see him and be intimidated by his ferocity.

Back at her desk, Veronica opened the instant message screen on her computer and typed, "Tink: Better call Mr. Graham (Texas American Bank) Pronto. He's hot...today's headlines. 449-7829. D'Angelo 12:07 PM"

Veronica began typing the Business Barometer Weekly Calendar of Events.The Calendar of Events was two hours past deadline. The People Column was due in less than an hour and it was not ready yet; Veronica still had over two hundred press releases to sift through just from this week's mail alone. The pile was enormous. She felt overwhelmed, and dreaded reading even one more sentence about all the businessmen and women in the Dallas Metro area promoted from resident nobody to "Sr. Almost Somebody." Veronica could only use promotions of Vice President and above, which made it difficult when she had to tell a secretary that her boss' press release would not be mentioned in the People Column when the secretary called to find out when it would run.

When Veronica took this job in the newsroom, she had hoped to become a reporter, but after six months on the job, she had begun to question her goal. Still, she admired Greg Tinkham and his hard-hitting style. Especially since one of his stories on the FDIC Savings and Loan bailout had been short-listed for the Pulitzer Prize three months ago. Although he didn't win, his status was definitely elevated in the newsroom because of it. Veronica often found excuses to talk to him, asking him questions about how he found his leads, his instinct for sniffing out a story. She admired him and wanted to learn all she could from him.

Veronica looked down at her fingers flying across the keyboard at a rate of 82 words per minute and noticed that her nails needed new polish. Her computer beeped and a message prompt flashed across her instant message screen.

"Veronica: If you can slow down long enough to eat, I'll be glad to buy your lunch. 15 minutes too early?" Tinkham. 12:14 pm.

For so long she'd waited for this invitation, but now she was on deadline. She couldn't go. She instant messaged him back, "Sounds great Greg, but I'm swamped. Rain check?" D'Angelo. 12:14 pm.

Across the newsroom, she could see Greg's arms shoot up in the air in an I-give-up manner.

Why is he so theatrical? He really should be on stage.

Just as she thought she'd missed her chance, he wrote back, "Your wish is my command fair lady…some time next week?" Tinkham 12:15 pm.

She watched Greg turn back around and grab his phone. He stood up and began another performance, already enthralled in a new conversation, no doubt trying to coerce or cajole his way into another front page story.

Veronica typed in a quick reply, "You bet Tink, thanks for the invite." D'Angelo 12:15 pm. Now she had something to look forward to: lunch with Tink. She'd make a list of questions to ask him. She smiled, thinking how this could turn into a very fortuitous lunch

Veronica had just a few more seminars to enter and then the weekly

Calendar of Events would be complete. But the phone suddenly erupted like a volcano, four lines at once. She answered the first call and asked if the caller could hold, but the caller refused to hold; instead he let loose a high pressured stream of self-importance and pompous hot air. Veronica punched the hold button in spite of his insistence that he speak to the editor immediately, then she routed the other calls to the respective reporters and took a message on the last call.

The phone rang again and this time it was the evening copy editor calling in sick. So just like that, Veronica was off deadline. The calendar could wait until tomorrow. The People column could wait too for that matter.

She messaged Greg back: "Cancel that rain-check…hunger pains are killing me…front elevator – 10 minutes?" D'Angelo 12:20 pm.

Greg signaled a thumbs-up from his desk without even turning around.

Greg held the elevator door, allowing Veronica to exit first. They walked into the subdued marble tiled lobby of the Dallas Times Herald and out into the downtown traffic noise. It was a warm day, with a cloudless sky and a gentle breeze. They crossed the street and walked in the cool shade of the blue-mirrored skyscrapers.

"So did you call Mr. Graham back?" asked Veronica.

Greg walked a few more steps in measured silence. He stuck his thumbs in his red suspenders, one of his many peculiar habits that Veronica found amusing.

"Nope," he said. "Been really busy this morning; I can feel another bank closure. It's on the verge. We're riding the crest of the wickedest tidal wave in FDIC history."

Veronica laughed. "Sick 'em mad dog."

He snarled. Then let out a rather loud growl. Several women walking ahead of them turned around to look. His infamous tear-apart savage reporting style had earned him the knick-name "mad dog" and he wore it like a medal of valor.

Tink, as he liked to be called, was an original. His faded hush puppy shoes, and his tan corduroy Levi's made his lower half seem pretty bland to Veronica. But his paisley print shirt and his red suspenders begged for attention. He kept his beard neatly trimmed, but his hair was always unruly, sticking out in all directions. Even his wire rim octagon glasses looked as if he borrowed them from someone else, twenty years ago.

"It's amazing how sensitive these bank executives are," he said. "Especially when they see their financial empires crumbling beneath their third world bad debt and their real estate fiascos."

"What happens to them when they need an FDIC bail-out? Don't they have any sort of accountability? Or can they just find some obscure Sr. Vice President job in another city?"

"Oh, they swim off shore and drown in their sorrows with all their other displaced shark friends," he said, popping his suspenders. "Then, like you said, they drift into another financial institution. Unless the government can file charges of criminal misconduct; then they do a little time at a country club federal prison. But that rarely happens."

"It just doesn't seem fair," said Veronica. "These men can throw away people's entire life savings, yet there's no recourse. Nothing happens to them except they lose their job. And all because they're too greedy. They take on bad debts at exorbitant interest rates, far too unrealistic to ever be repaid, so they fold."

"That's simplifying it a little," he said.

"Simple or not, there ought to be a way to hold them accountable for their greed."

"It's not greed that motivates these people," said Greg. They paused on the corner to wait for the light to change. "It's a quest for power. Like I read in college, way back in my PSYCH 101, the quest for power drives much of man's social actions."

Veronica considered this for a moment. "I think that an insecure person, no matter what his culture, will show the same general characteristics, like an eagerness for power."

Greg laughed. "So these guys running around burying the financial community do it out of insecurity?"

Veronica shrugged. She considered Greg to be an ace reporter and a nice guy, but one who didn't always know as much as the thought he did, outside of the banking field that is. "Oh who knows," she said. "Do you think Dick will come back after lunch today?"

"Good question. One never knows with Dick," he said. "But that's one of the perks of being the Big Guy. No one tells the editor when to be at his desk and when to be at a meeting."

The museum café was only two more blocks up ahead. Veronica's shoes were rubbing a blister on the back of her heel. She bent down and adjusted the strap and someone stuck a booklet in her face. She looked up and an old man carrying an armload of green pamphlets said, "Go ye in peace and power," and walked away.

"What the hell?" Greg asked, reaching for the pamphlet. He read from the cover, "How We Can All Get Rich..."

He opened the pamphlet and flipped through the pages. Then he gave it back to her.

She opened the cover and read the title page, "How We Can All Get Rich! is a plain tale of common sense and GREAT ENLIGHTENMENT, written in a Beautiful Way for Wise People of All Ages and Races who are in All Nations and Places, by a Humble Man with the Power of Persuasion!"

"Just what we need," said Greg. "Another humble man with the power of persuasion." He took the pamphlet back from her, folded it and threw it in the trash.

They walked up to the entrance of the museum and into the café filled with elderly women, and blue-suited office workers who occupied the downtown offices during business hours. Against the sea of navy blue suits and silk power ties, Greg's red suspenders stood out.

They moved through the line, ordered their food and took a table by the window with a great metropolitan view. The waiter brought them hot fresh bread.

"So tell me," Greg said. "What's an intelligent, beautiful, and charming girl like you doing at the Business Desk?"

Veronica chewed her bread and considered how to answer that question. Studying journalists? Honing my writing skills? Or just being my intelligent, beautiful and charming self?

"Paying rent."

"Yeah, but you could make a lot more money as an executive secretary somewhere else, couldn't you?"

"The last thing I want to be is a secretary," she said.

"Then why'd you take this administrative assistant position on the Business Desk?"

Veronica took a swallow of iced tea and wondered why reporters always talk to you as if they are interviewing you.

"When Dick hired me," she said slowly, "He told me he wanted to expand the responsibilities of the position and change the title to Editorial Assistant. He said that I would eventually be doing some writing, so it sounded appealing."

"Oh," Greg said. "So you want to write?"

"I thought I did," she said, twisting the mauve linen napkin in her lap and thinking about her weekly 'Calendar of Events' and her ridiculous 'People and Promotions' column. "But I'm not really sure that journalism is the right field for me. The longer I work in the newsroom, the more I realize that I like to make up stories, not dig for them."

He laughed. "I didn't know you had an interest in creative writing. I once fancied myself as a writer."

"What happened?" she asked.

"Life."

She watched him as he added two packages of sugar to his iced tea. He stirred, thinking for a moment then said, "I needed to earn a decent living. So reporting jumped up and grabbed me. My wife always used to find reasons why I should earn more money. She's good at finding reasons why I should do lots of things."

Veronica imagined Greg at home being nagged by his wife and decided to change the subject.

"Do you like your job?" she asked.

He didn't answer her.

"Lots of people in that newsroom hate their jobs, and they're very vocal about it," she said.

"I don't hate my job at all," he said. "I just wish there weren't so many copy editors breathing down my neck, waiting to get their hands on my work to delete, add to, or otherwise alter my stories."

"Like your Texas American Bank story?" she asked.

"Exactly," he said. "Those T.A.B. people are irate now: just think what they'd be doing if Dick had left it alone and let it run the way I wrote it."

"They'd probably be trying to have you arrested," she said. She remembered thinking yesterday when she first read the story that she wished she had written it. She really admired Tink and the way he wrote.

Veronica waved to the waiter. She wanted to order more tea. Greg continued his professional self-analysis and the more he talked the more Veronica began to see him in a new light. He was fairly arrogant and she thought it funny how she'd never noticed this before.

"Reporters affect things, make waves. What we say has repercussions. We're supposed to tell the facts and sometimes certain facts can move mountains."

Veronica drank the last of her tea in one big gulp. She didn't want to hear any more about moving mountains and making waves.

"A person either creates or destroys; there is no neutrality," he said.

She looked over her shoulder for the waiter. She wanted more tea.

"Seize the Day," Greg said. "It's from Saul Bellow's 'Seize the Day.' Depending on how much power you have, you might create or destroy a whole lot. Power is a wonderful thing in the hands of those who know how to use it."

The waiter finally arrived with more tea. Greg ordered two glasses of Chablis. Veronica stared at him.

"What's wrong?" he asked. "You don't like it when a man orders for you?"

"I really shouldn't drink and then go back to the office and try to type," she said.

"Then don't go back to the office," he said. "Run off with me to a secret hide away."

She looked at him. He smiled. She couldn't decide if she should be offended or flattered.

"We could take a room at the Fairmont and disappear for the afternoon."

"Yeah right," Veronica said, nearly choking. She assumed Greg either had no concept of couth, or was too conceited to realize how disgusting he sounded.

"You might be glad you did," he said, still smiling.

He looked somehow different to Veronica now. Repulsive. No longer the quirky, amusing, eccentric yet halfway decent guy that made her laugh.

She wanted to slap his smug little smile clear off his face. But she wasn't sure how he'd react. She'd never slapped a man before. What if he hit her back?

"Maybe we should invite your wife?" she said coolly. She turned her head and stared at a small sparrow fluttering by the window as it built its nest in the over hang of the roof.

"I know I have nothing to offer you. You're young, attractive and vivacious. I'm none of those things, but I can't help desiring you. Can't you just..."

"Really Greg!" she said, shifting her gaze back to him. "Don't you think we ought to drop it? I'm not the type that has flings with married men. And even if I was, it's still not a very good idea."

"Why not?" he asked.

She folded her napkin and laid it purposefully over her plate. This meal was finished.

"Let me explain something about myself," she said, having no idea what she was about to explain.

He reached for her untouched glass of Chablis. He raised it as if to toast her.

"There's nothing to explain," he said, still smiling. "I made you an offer. You declined it. No need to analyze why. I respect your decision, and I won't try to change your mind. But if you ever decide to reconsider, don't hesitate to let me know."

He signaled the waiter for the check.

She shut her eyes and tried to convince herself that this wasn't happening. Veronica thought surely as intelligent as Greg was, he couldn't possibly believe that she found him irresistible. Or could he? Or was this just his way of trying to manipulate her? Did he honestly think she would allow him to do that to her?

Maybe this was how he manipulated his wife into marrying him and now she repays him by nagging.

"Will you excuse me please?" she said, not waiting for him to answer before she left. She hurried into the ladies' room, feeling her face flush.

"Veronica will you step into my office please?" Dick asked her over the intercom.

She hurried into Dick's office. He motioned to her to sit in the leather chair facing his desk. He stood, picked up the message she had left on his phone and walked over to his door. He shut the door slowly.

"This Mr. Graham fellow," he said. "When he called, did he actually use the word liar?"

"Yes. He called Greg a liar, and accused him of fabricating quotes."

Dick sat down on the edge of his desk. "And what time did this call come in?"

She told him she took this particular message around noon, but a woman from Texas American Bank called several times earlier this morning. She told him she took three messages but Greg did not return her calls.

Dick grunted. He walked around to his chair and sat down slowly and with much gravity of purpose; like a retired judge, called back to the bench to rule on a landmark case.

"So he actually called Greg a liar, with little or no integrity?"

"Yes. He was speaking pretty fast, but I copied it down as best I could."

"Well, I appreciate your effort," he said. "Did Greg happen to mention why he wouldn't return Mr. Graham's call?"

She told him that Greg had been tied up with Fisher on the First Republic story all morning. "He asked me to hold all his calls early this morning since he had a lot to do today."

She hoped that would get him in trouble. Would he be put on probation? Would there be some kind of investigation into whether he manipulated the facts?

"He certainly has had some breaking stories all at once here lately," Dick said.

The phone rang. Dick did not make a move to answer it.

"Do you want me to grab that?" she asked.

"No," he said. "I'll take it myself. That's all I needed," he said. "But if Mr. Graham calls again, or anyone else from Texas American Bank, then interrupt me wherever I am."

"Okay," she said. She shut the door behind her then took the long way back to her desk, avoiding the vicinity of Tinkham's work area.

She sat down at her desk and began typing. The phone rang and she answered it.

"Let me talk to the editor!" said a graveled husky voice.

"I'm sorry, he's on another call. May I take a message?"

"No!" he yelled at her. "But maybe you can tell me why you allow Safeway to sell your newspaper and charge a sales tax."

"Excuse me?" said Veronica.

"You heard me!" he screamed into the phone. "Why are they charging a sales tax when the city just passed a law outlawing sales tax on newspapers? Can't you answer me," he said, "or do you not give a shit?"

Stunned, Veronica glanced up at the clock. She was so completely unprepared for this outburst that she could not collect her thoughts enough to tell this caller that if he would bother to read the paper, he would know that the law the city council passed was actually enacting a mandatory sales tax on newspapers in order to raise revenues for the rapid transit debt.

"Can't you answer me?" he yelled. "Don't you know anything or do you just not give a fuck?"

Veronica tried to force the words out of her mouth, but only a weak whimper issued forth. "Now just a minute," she said, but the caller hung up on her.

She didn't care what her job description said; she shouldn't have to put up with obscene and abusive phone calls. She ran into the ladies room, so angry she was close to tears.

She returned to her desk to find the publisher, the managing editor, Dick Heath and Greg Tinkham gathered in posse in the center of the newsroom just a few feet from her desk. Dick made his point succinctly and with a glib flair for poise under pressure. Even if he was blatantly wrong on an issue, he could convince you that he was right simply with his talent for persuasive speech.

"I defended Tinkham to the very end," Dick said to the publisher. "In no way did Tinkham libel Texas American or its officials. He simply stated the facts, and if the facts cause a panic, and a run on deposits, then the facts are serious and need to be in print."

"But..." said the publisher, trying to sift through the conflicting stories. "Graham is saying that the run on deposits during the last three weeks has cleared $800 million, requiring FDIC aid. And if these massive withdrawals were caused by erroneous reporting, then we are definitely libel."

"Excuse me sir," Tinkham butted in, "But at no time did I state anything contrary to the factual data supplied to me by Texas American's own staff. If there are erroneous stats, then they made the errors themselves. I quoted their stats word for word."

The publisher continued, saying he understood, but as a journalist Tink was obligated to not abuse his power of free speech. He indicated that Tink, Dick and even he was responsible for each and every printed word so it simply must be accurate. He checked his watch then said, "I'm late for another meeting, gentlemen, so if you'll excuse me, I'm sure you can clear this matter up. If you'll just talk to Mr. Graham yourself, Greg."

He left, with the managing editor following at his heels. Dick turned to Tinkham, "We'll support you on this, Tink."

Tinkham looked at Veronica for a brief moment, until she picked up the phone, pretending to be making a call to verify the times for an investment seminar for the calendar of events.

Tinkham stalked out of the newsroom. Veronica hung up the phone.

After several hours of steady typing, her hands were beginning to cramp. She watched the clock anxiously awaiting the five-thirty signal for freedom. Only forty-five more minutes to go.

The phone rang and Veronica answered it.

"Hello," said a raspy voice.

"Yes? Can I help you?" she asked.

"I hope so," said the caller. His voice sounded muffled, yet it reminded her of someone she knew. She started to speak, but then glanced at the switchboard. Her line was lit up, and the only other line lit up was Greg Tinkham's.

She glanced at Greg's desk. He wasn't standing or gesturing. His back was towards Veronica, and he was hunched way down over his desk. Maybe his wife was on the phone nagging him again.

"Look," Veronica said, "If you need to speak to someone at the business desk, then tell me who it is."

The caller hung up. Veronica reached over to hang up the phone and noticed that Greg's phone line was no longer lit up. He was sitting at his desk, motionless. He straightened his back, sitting as erect as possible without standing up.

The next time the phone rang Veronica glanced at the switchboard and noticed that Tinkham's line was engaged. The phone rang again and she ignored it. It rang three more times and she stopped typing. The phone continued to ring and the airline industry reporter looked up from her desk as if to see why Veronica had not yet answered the phone.

Finally, Veronica picked up the phone.

"Hello?" said that same raspy voice, after a few brief moments of heavy breathing.

Veronica didn't say anything. She pushed the disconnect button and immediately Tink's line flashed off at the same time as hers. She turned off her computer and her desk lamp and she watched Tink slip further down in his seat, only the top of his head visible from where she stood.

She was amazed that Tinkham, for all his skill and prowess as a reporter, didn't have even the most basic understanding of how a multiline phone system worked as he apparently had no clue that Veronica could see when he was on the phone. She stood up, gathering her coat and purse. Disgusted, she shook her head and walked out of the newsroom.

Savannah, Pierre and the Piano

Chewing her gum and swinging her hips, Savannah hurried up the sidewalk to the front entrance of Red Hills Nursing Home. She waved to several of her friends, fellow members of her church youth group, who were also just arriving. They met outside the double glass doors and chatted excitedly while letting their dogs tug at their leashes and get acquainted. This was the first "Pet Therapy Session" for Savannah and her friends.

Although only fourteen, Savannah could easily pass for nineteen or twenty. Her mother said she had 'filled out a lot' for her age. Savannah used to be self-conscious about her body but lately she'd become more comfortable with it. Consequently she received frequent attention from the opposite gender. Savannah had freckles, blue eyes and ash blond hair, which she repeatedly checked in the mirror. She could be simultaneously bubbly, insecure, self-absorbed, opinionated, and full of nervous energy. And at times she could be extraordinarily kind.

This was Savannah's first experience in community service projects. Likewise, none of the other members of this youth group had ever done anything like this. The project was the brainchild of Amanda Taylor, the church's youth director. By 2:00 p.m., seven teenagers and their pets had converged on the nursing home, in order to spend one hour of their time visiting shut-ins.

Savannah wrinkled her nose upon entering the lobby. "Oh gross. It smells like pee in here."

Mrs. Daily, a frail wisp of a woman, sat stooped in an overstuffed chair beside the grand piano. A quilted pad carefully folded beneath her covered the upholstery. Her hands were gnarled and her knuckles knobby and arthritic.

Mrs. Daily sighed. She was proud. Refined. And held her eyes erect even though her spine was humped. She sat in the lobby every Sunday afternoon next to the piano and imagined herself fifty years ago, performing in symphony halls across the country. Mrs. Daily closed her eyes and heard Rachmaninoff, Beethoven, Debussy. Today she had also heard the comment, so carelessly flung from Savannah's glossed lips.

Savannah swished through the lobby with her mother's apricot colored toy poodle, Pierre, pulling at the end of his rhinestone studded silver leash. Mrs. Daily opened one eye, surprised, and then she glanced around at all the teenagers and their dogs. She recalled her own precious Ludwig and his velvety Dachshund ear trembling under her thumb as she fingered the corner of her urine stained pad beneath her skirt. However, that tenderness existed only as a memory. Ludwig had passed on many years ago.

A small beagle named Rosebud, started to hyperventilate. Rosebud's fourteen-year-old owner, Josh, bent down and stroked her head.

"Oh my gosh! How totally gross!" Savannah squealed. "What's wrong with him?"

"She's a girl. And beagles just do this when they get excited." Josh gazed up at Savannah, but his eyes did not make it past her tight knit tank top.

"That's disgusting," Savannah whined, pulling Pierre's leash in order to keep her dog away from Rosebud, as if the condition were contagious. "Make him quit, I can't stand to hear that awful sound."

Josh stroked Rosebud's neck then picked up the dog in his arms. "She can't help it. Besides, it'll stop in a minute."

Anxious to escape the torturous noise, Savannah hurried across the lobby to greet Kevin as he strolled through the front entrance. Kevin was the only member of the group who did not bring a pet. He came to "observe," as he told Amanda. Kevin was tall and thin. He wore his sandy blond hair cut short on top and shoulder length in back. He wore a plaid shirt and faded jeans with hiking boots. He looked clean but slightly rumpled.

Though she had no children of her own, Amanda understood the kids in her youth group far better than any of them realized. So Amanda knew Kevin's sole reason for attending this community service event was purely self-motivated; spending an hour with Savannah was what truly mattered. Amanda did not hold this against him because she knew that regardless of his reasons for attending, he might be able to gain some valuable experience. As soon as Kevin stepped into the lobby, Savannah rushed up to him, greeting him with breathless accounts of this strange place and its foul odors.

"Gheeze. Look at all those wheelchairs and walkers lined up in the lobby. How're we supposed to get our dogs organized with that stuff in the way? And can you believe how smelly it is here? Yuck. Oh and, will you hold Pierre a minute? I've got to find the ladies room." She gathered the poodle into her arms and passed him to Kevin. He grinned as the back of his hand brushed against Savannah's breast. He took the dog then watched with pleasure as she scurried down the corridor.

Inside the ladies room, Savannah glanced at herself in the mirror. She flicked a stray strand of ash blond hair out of her blue eyes. She patted down her bangs then smoothed out the creases in her lip gloss. Satisfied with the moist sheen, she hurried into the stall and shut the door. She thought about Kevin, humming softly as she chewed her gum.

Kevin waited in the lobby, holding Pierre. The dog reeked of perfume. Kevin held it at arm's length, then set it down on the floor and stood on the silver studded leash. His thick-soled hiking boots were caked with dried mud along the edges. He closed his eyes, remembering the dream he had last night about Savannah. It was his first wet dream and it embarrassed him to recall the arousing dream here in a nursing home.

Kevin wondered why Savannah always took so long in the ladies room. He inadvertently ground the rhinestone studs into the tile floor beneath his boot as he gazed around the lobby.

Rushing out of the ladies room, Savannah accidentally bumped into Amanda, almost knocking her off balance. Attempting to sidestep the girl's clumsy emergence from the powder room, Amanda laughed out loud saying, "Hey there little miss human canon ball." She touched her hand to

Savannah's shoulder, "Ready to go?"

Savannah nodded, giggled and then blew a bubble. They walked in silence down the hallway to the front lobby where a cacophony of barks, growls, and yelps hung in the air. Amanda pressed her fingers tight against her teeth and whistled. Even the dogs looked up at her and simultaneously silenced their yapping.

"Okay guys. Are we ready to start?" Amanda glanced around at her charges. The kids nodded. "Let's start at the far end of the hallway." Tails wagged. Toenails clicked across hard, cold tiles as they moved en masse to the long corridor. They converged at the nurse's station like a pack of nervous greyhounds at the starting gate. Amanda took her own dog, Gypsy, and led the entourage. Curious and quiet, they followed Amanda into the A wing.

Glancing over her shoulder, Amanda caught a glimpse of Savannah batting her long lashes at Kevin. "Okay, gather round for a sec," Amanda said, motioning for them to come closer.

The kids huddled around her.

"Now remember," she said softly, tugging on Gypsy's leash so that the dog sat at her feet immediately with that single, non-verbal command. "We are about to enter these people's home so please mind your manners."

Ignoring Amanda's admonishment, Savannah giggled as Kevin took her hand and placed it in his back pocket.

Amanda saw this but chose not to address it. She had spoken to them before about public display of affection. They were constantly holding hands. Even during the church service. Just last week, while passing the offering plate, Amanda had seen Savannah wrap her ankle around Kevin's foot underneath the pew. However, Amanda secretly delighted in the budding romance occurring as if under her tutelage yet she knew part of her responsibility as youth director was to instill socially acceptable behavior parameters for her students.

Savannah giggled again. Kevin then slapped his hand over her mouth. Of course Amanda saw the fire in Savannah's eyes and knew that anything she said about their affection would fall on deaf ears. Amanda desperately hoped this afternoon would create an element of empathy in her kids, and broaden their scope of awareness a bit.

At the end of the hall they found a room marked "Group Activities." A big screen TV dominated the room. Several rockers and wheelchairs fanned out in a semi-circle in front of the TV. Mrs. Gato sat alone in the corner. Her plastic cushion had slipped halfway out of her wheelchair, so that her body was contorted, leaning sideways over the armrest. Mrs. Gato wore a yellow headscarf, a bright red housecoat, and fuzzy green slippers. She smacked her lips, with the milky sound of a newborn pup giving suck. "Mlick. Mmmlick." She then presented the room with her gift of voluminous flatulence.

Looks of shock and amusement crept onto the faces of the youth volunteers while their dogs, on the other hand, tugged at their leashes, sniffing, exploring, and wagging their tails at the sight of so many new faces. When Mrs. Gato saw the kids enter with their dogs, her eyes widened. She knew she had an audience now, so she screamed, "Help! Help! Help!" until Amanda approached her, reaching out slowly then gently touching her bony shoulder.

"Hi there," Amanda said, as she helped return the old woman to an upright position and readjusted her plastic cushion. Amanda then took a throw pillow from the empty couch in back, and wedged it in between Mrs. Gato and the armrest of her wheelchair.

"Would you like to feed my dog?" Amanda asked, smiling. Mrs. Gato glanced up, uncertain at first, and then slowly held out her trembling hand. Amanda pulled several dog treats from the plastic baggie in her pocket and dropped three small biscuits into the woman's wrinkled palm. Mrs. Gato timidly held out a treat for Gypsy. The dog bit into it gingerly at first, then crunched it up with relish as crumbs dropped into the nappy fuzz of Mrs. Gato's lime green house slippers. Amanda knelt beside Gypsy, stroking her head as she chewed, then glanced up at Mrs. Gato just in time to see her put one of the dog treats into her own mouth. Amanda then heard a sudden gasp behind her, and looked back to see Savannah, eyes wide, gawking at Mrs. Gato.

Savannah's hand flew to her mouth, covering her gaping disgust. Amanda looked away, struggling with whether or not to stop this woman from eating a "doggie treat." Savannah glanced at Amanda, as if begging her to take that nasty dog food away from this crazy old lady before she ate any more of it. Amanda ignored Savannah's reaction.

After visiting with all the residents in the Group Activities Room, the kids took their pets to the room across the hallway, where the door stood wide open. While the rest of the group waited in the hallway, Amanda, Savannah and Kevin knocked on the open door then entered the room.

Mr. Stone lay motionless on his hospital bed, staring at the ceiling. Mr. Stone's grandson was sitting in a chair beside the bed, watching a golf tournament on TV. He rose as the kids entered the room, and motioned for them to come inside after Amanda explained their pet therapy visit. The grandson explained that Mr. Stone had recently had a stroke which had left him partially paralyzed and unable to speak clearly. Mr. Stone turned his head to see the kids and their dogs entering the room. His eyes filled with tears when they approached his bed. Savannah watched as Amanda moved closer and carefully lifted her dog up above the steel safety rails.

Amanda bent down eye level with Mr. Stone and gently patted his right hand. Gypsy's tan fur with its white markings on her back and paws gave her the appearance of a fawn. As meek and passive as a baby deer, Gypsy was sleek and streamlined, bred for speed with her sculpted well-defined muscular hind legs.

"This is Gypsy. She's an Italian greyhound. A miniature breed. She's full grown and weighs twelve pounds." Gypsy licked Mr. Stone's left hand. He clutched the metal railing. His milky gray eyes focused on the dog as a single tear spilled from the corner of his left eye.

This hit Savannah harder than a sudden slap in her face. She pulled a tissue from her pocket, deposited her gum in the tissue then tossed it into the trashcan by the door as she left Mr. Stone's room. Her smile vanished. Her bubbliness dissipated. Simply because she had witnessed this unexpected gesture of reciprocated contact. She couldn't handle this anymore. She told Amanda she felt faint and needed to step outside for some fresh air. She said she would wait up front in the "piano room" for the rest of the group to finish. She left quickly, not waiting for Kevin to follow her. As he was busy talking with Mr. Stone's grandson by the TV, Kevin did not even notice Savannah had gone.

Upon returning to the lobby, Savannah saw Mrs. Daily hunched over like a gargoyle with her claw-like hands resting on her knees. Savannah hesitated then took Pierre over to visit Mrs. Daily. The old woman's entire demeanor changed when she saw Pierre. She beamed at the dog then reached down to pet him, gently stroking his apricot curls. She laughed then asked Savannah if she played the piano, and Savannah replied, "Yes. But I only know one song. *Twinkle Twinkle Little Star.*"

"Good," replied Mrs. Daily. "Let's hear it."

Savannah two-fingered the lullaby then Pierre jumped up in Mrs. Daily's lap and licked her face. Mrs. Daily laughed and cooed and cawed at Pierre, calling him *Ludwig* over and over. No longer smacking her gum or fiddling with her hair, no longer the center of her own short attention span, had Savannah watched in silence as Mrs. Daily fondled Pierre's ears.

"Play it again," said Mrs. Daily, smiling broadly.

Savannah obliged, playing the one tune she knew over and over for almost twenty minutes until a sudden loud wheezing sound startled her from behind. She turned to see Rosebud tugging at the end of her leash as Josh tried in vain to control his dog and make her heel. When Savannah glanced back at Mrs. Daily, she noticed a drop of fluid dangling on the tip of her wrinkled nose.

Savannah closed her eyes, just for a moment. Then she reached into her hip pocket and pulled out a fresh tissue. She held it out for Mrs. Daily, but the old woman did not see it. She was too absorbed in stroking Pierre. Savannah looked back over her shoulder at Kevin who had just walked up behind her. He raised one eyebrow, clearly no help. He shrugged, shoved his hands in his pockets then wandered off toward the front door.

Savannah leaned down beside Mrs. Daily and whispered, "Would you like to blow your nose, Ma'am?" Mrs. Daily's foggy gray eyes meandered over toward Savannah's steady ice blue gaze.

"Of course, dear, go ahead." Mrs. Daily craned her face up towards Savannah.

Savannah hesitated then gently pressed the tissue to Mrs. Daily's nose. After she finished helping Mrs. Daily blow her nose, she stood up and took a deep breath. She did not giggle or wonder about her hair. She touched Mrs. Daily's shoulder and said, "I'll leave some tissues with you, just in case you need more."

Savannah pulled a flattened packet of tissues from her back pocket and placed them on the stained pad beside Mrs. Daily. Savannah took Pierre from Mrs. Daily's arms, and whispered to him, "Go find Kevin!" The dog scampered off, wagging its tail, and found Kevin standing alone, gazing out the front window.

Savannah watched Kevin as he stood by the entrance. She did not giggle or swish as she approached him. Savannah was fourteen yet she suddenly felt strangely foreign to her youth. Her thoughts were filled with images of Mr. Stone crying, of Mrs. Daily clutching Pierre, and of Mrs. Gato eating a dog biscuit. Savannah felt uneasy, yet she continued forward, approaching Kevin as he stood aloof by the exit, engrossed in his own reaction to the afternoon visitation.

Savannah immediately saw herself in Mrs. Daily's place. Alone at eighty-eight years old. She saw Kevin prone in a hospital bed, paralyzed by a stroke like Mr. Stone. And she did this all in a split second, her eyes still locked on Kevin.

Quietly, she walked up behind Kevin and touched him on the shoulder. She then took Pierre's leash from his hand. They stepped outside into the sunlight, away from the ethereal isolation they'd both experienced inside, and they followed behind Pierre as he sniffed at the manicured shrubbery. Savannah stopped suddenly and grabbed Kevin's belt loop, pulling him back to her.

"Do you think I'm pretty?" she asked him, her voice shaky. She glanced up at him then down at the sidewalk, clearly ashamed of feeling the need to ask such an inane question. Kevin laughed aloud, a little bit nervous, embarrassed by her discomfort. She looked up at him, the terror in her eyes now obvious, even to Kevin. In a moment of compassion he took her face in his hands, leaned down and kissed her on the lips. She smiled as he kissed her on the tip of her nose, her forehead, then on her eyelids as she slowly shut her eyes.

When Kevin put his nervous hand on her hip, her eyes opened at once, locking him in her rigid gaze. "Will you think I'm pretty in fifty years?" she asked.

Kevin laughed. Then just as abruptly he stopped laughing. He remembered the urine smell, the woman crying, "Help! Help!" and the paralysis of Mr. Stone. He hesitated then suddenly grabbed Savannah's hand and drew her closer to him. He wrapped his arms around her, pinning her hands behind her, nestled in the small of her arched back. Kevin bent down; lips parted, and found the welcoming warmth of her tongue against his.

It was their first French kiss. He felt certain it must be her first time. Her body tensed with apprehension and longing.

She would never forget this moment, because it would never be the same again. This moment and its incredible awakening.

Standing by the double glass doors, Amanda had seen everything. Clearly understanding the clumsy mechanics of their embrace, she remembered her own awkward first kiss so many years ago. She smiled, watching them through the window without the slightest bit of embarrassment, not once shying away from this accidental voyeurism.

A moment later, Mrs. Daily's cackling laughter popped this shiny little memory bubble, pulling Amanda back into the present to the antiseptic and urine smell of the lobby, to the muffled sighs of the elderly. Mrs. Daily laughed again, then lifted her hand to her lips and blew a kiss to the crowd. Carnegie Hall never felt so good. Amanda strolled up to Mrs. Daily and for the first time noticed the tattered, yellowed sheet music Mrs. Daily clutched in her twisted fingers. Beethoven's *Fur Elise*. Amanda could still play this from memory, so many hours it had taken to perfect it all those years ago. She had performed it at her piano recital in seventh grade and she still remembered the moment on stage when she finished playing and she stood up to take a bow, loving the applause of the audience.

Amanda took the sheet music from Mrs. Daily and approached the piano, touching her forefinger to the jet black, highly polished mahogany. She sat down, took a deep breath, and began to play. Beethoven's notes spiraled up off the taut baby grand strings. Swirling. Dancing. Whirling and floating up high to the ceiling. Lighter than air bubbles underwater. Lighter even than helium in a balloon, the music lifted the entire lobby and all its inhabitants upward to the frenzied apex.

Mrs. Daily stared at Amanda as she played, her dewy eyes barely focusing on the curve of Amanda's chin or the wisp of hair in Amanda's eyes. Mrs. Daily grinned, her thin dry lips stretching tight over her loose dentures. Taking one of Savannah's tissues, Mrs. Daily dabbed at her eyes, relaxing back into the plush chair, reveling in the memories of such sweet, sweet music.

Mrs. Daily closed her eyes, thinking to herself that dying right now would be more pleasant than living another day without at last hearing this music once again.

Suddenly, Gypsy let out a loud, lamentable howl. Amanda looked up. Her hands dropped to the keys in a discordant thud. She jumped up and ran to Mrs. Daily who had slouched in her chair. The old woman's left arm hung down limp over the armrest. Her mouth gaped open and her eyes rolled up in her head.

Amanda put her cheek up against Mrs. Daily's face, and could feel no breath. She grabbed Mrs. Daily's dangling wrist and felt no pulse. She hesitated only a second or two then backed away two steps. She then turned and ran to the nurses' station while Beethoven's music crescendoed in her ears, louder and louder as Gypsy sat at Mrs. Daily's feet and continued to howl, with such sadness and grief that it sounded almost human.

Amanda approached the charge nurse and told her that Mrs. Daily had stopped breathing. The charge nurse immediately asked the aide to call 911, and then the nurse ran down the hallway to the lobby. Amanda followed right behind her.

Gypsy was sitting at Mrs. Daily's feet, still howling. Amanda grabbed her dog out of the way then helped the charge nurse lay Mrs. Daily out on the floor so she could perform CPR.

After only a few brief moments, the charge nurse was able to revive Mrs. Daily. Amanda ran back to the nurse's station to get a blanket to prevent Mrs. Daily from going into shock. Mrs. Daily cleared her throat, coughed a few times then asked if she could play her Beethoven Sonata No. 2 as her encore number after the standing ovation.

The charge nurse took Mrs. Daily's wrist, feeling for a pulse.

"I think you've just had a heart attack, Mrs. Daily. We'll be taking you to the hospital as soon as the ambulance arrives."

Amanda returned with the blanket and covered Mrs. Daily's legs and torso.

Mrs. Daily said, "I wanted to die just now, rich with the sound of Beethoven in my ears, rich with applause from Carnegie Hall. Why didn't you let me die in peace?"

The nurse replied, "I can't just let you die. That's in God's hands."

Mrs. Daily started to cry. "But I've lived long enough. And it is my dying wish to hear Beethoven as I pass on."

The charge nurse held Mrs. Daily's hand and said, "Lie still now."

Then paramedics arrived momentarily and after they loaded Mrs. Daily into the ambulance, Amanda got in her car and started to leave until she saw Savannah standing on the corner with Pierre. Amanda got out of her car and approached Savannah.

"What happened? Where's your ride?" Amanda asked.

"My sister called and said she was still at the movies and she won't be able to pick me up for another hour."

"I'll take you home," said Amanda. "There's no need for you to wait that long."

"Oh, thank you," Savannah said. "I should have let Kevin's mom give me a ride when she offered, but that was before my sister called and said she'd be an hour late."

"Come on," said Amanda, "Let's go."

On the way home Amanda said, "It's a shame you started feeling sick this afternoon. I was so hoping you kids would enjoy this so we could do it on a regular basis, maybe once a month or something like that."

Savannah nodded.

"Mrs. Daily had a heart attack," Amanda said, "That's why the ambulance came."

"Which one was Mrs. Daily?" asked Savannah.

"The woman sitting by herself, next to the piano."

"She had a heart attack? I played Twinkle Twinkle Little Star for her about fifty times. Is she okay?"

"She's on her way to the hospital."

"I wonder if she has any family," said Savannah. "Wouldn't it be awful to get that old and not have any family?"

Amanda said, "It would be very difficult without family to help you."

"Do you think we could go see her in the hospital?"

Amanda glanced over at Savannah. "That's a fine idea, Savannah."

"She seemed so lonely, and she kept calling Pierre a strange name, Ludwig, or something like that."

"I'll call the hospital tomorrow to find out her condition then maybe we can visit her in the evening, if it's okay with your parents."

"Maybe Kevin can go too," said Savannah.

"I don't know about that," said Amanda. "Let's just you and I do it on our own."

"Do you not like Kevin, Amanda?"

"Of course I like him. I was merely considering what your parents would think if your church youth director started taking you and your boyfriend places."

"Oh, I see what you mean," said Savannah.

A silence settled between them as Amanda drove and Savannah stroked Pierre.

When they arrived at Savannah's home, Amanda said, "I'll call you tomorrow to let you know how Mrs. Daily is doing, and then we can decide what time to go visit her."

"Great. And thanks so much for the ride."

"Your welcome. Thank you for coming this afternoon, I think it was a success all around."

Savannah smiled, than shut the door. She held up Pierre's paw and waved goodbye to Amanda, then she ran up to the house.

As Amanda watched Savannah hurry up the sidewalk to her home, she felt a huge surge of emotion swelling up inside. It wasn't exactly grief or loneliness or the missing out on having a husband or a child; it was more like an unnamable sense of the transitory nature of life. Or the ubiquitous nature of death— surreptitious in its presence— marking each moment that passed as a small death in a way, since that moment would never exist again.

Amanda thought of Mrs. Daily, and her wish to hear Beethoven as she passed on. She thought of Kevin kissing Savannah, and she thought of Gypsy's howling when Mrs. Daily stopped breathing. Amanda looked down at her hands, eyeing the emptiness of her left hand— no wedding band or engagement ring— and she started to cry.

Just then Gypsy stood up on the seat next to Amanda and licked her right hand as she gripped the steering wheel.

It tickled.

Amanda laughed through her tears. She then picked up her little dog and hugged her tight, and drove home with Gypsy sitting in her lap.

On the Green Earth Contemplating the Moon

Maggie and Allison huddled around the sink in their couchette, washing their feet as the train pulled into the station. It was a custom they'd learned from an Indian woman in the restroom at JFK Airport. "Wash your feet before you arrive in a new city and leave behind whatever dirt and dust you've collected on your journey," said the Indian woman. "It will bring you luck."

It worked. Nimes, Marseille, Nice. The girls had tried it with each new city on this leg of their trip, and invariably they had met a local who took them to places they would never have found on their own.

It was June, 2008. Now they were in Monte Carlo with only a little over four hundred dollars left between them, but at least Maggie had her fiancé's credit card. It didn't take them long to find the Plaza Hotel. The rooms were expensive, but Maggie's fiancé had offered them his credit card in case they got into a bind.

"I feel guilty, using his Visa card when it's not exactly an emergency." Allison said.

"Don't worry about it," Maggie replied. "He can afford it. Besides, it makes him happy when he feels needed and appreciated."

Allison laughed. "I certainly appreciate him right now. I am so ready for a luxurious bathtub, aren't you?"

"Absolutely. Then let's hit the beaches," Maggie said.

"Okay Maggie. Sounds good to me."

The girls left the lobby, walked through the dining room and went outside to the veranda overlooking the beach.

"Check this out," Maggie said, gazing through a telescope. She pointed it down to the beach where a group of women lay sunbathing together. Allison bent down and looked through the scope. Several of the women were topless.

"Looks like an interesting beach," said Allison.

They left the veranda and headed for their room. They rode the mirrored elevator in silence, gazing at their reflection as they ascended to the eleventh floor.

They found their room, opened the door and were pleasantly surprised by all the velvet and satin.

"Far cry from the youth hostel circuit," Maggie said. She put her backpack on the bed and began unpacking her wrinkled clothes. She smoothed them out with her hands then put them away in the antique chest of drawers.

Allison unpacked the one dress that she had brought with her and hung it up in the armoire. It was a pale yellow crushed silk sundress, and a few new wrinkles didn't even show on it. That was precisely why she'd brought it on the trip.

"Let's eat out tonight at a fancy place," Allison said. "We can use your plastic, and when we get home, I'll pay you back."

Maggie agreed. "Why not," she said. "We deserve a treat, after all."

They bathed and changed into their swimsuits then hurried down to the beach before the afternoon sun waned too far behind the cliffs.

"Look at this beach," Allison said, stopping at the edge of the veranda to take off her tennis shoes. "It's not even real sand, it's just rocks."

Maggie sat in a deck chair, pulled off her shoes and stuffed them into the bag. "It's pretty though," she said. "I've never seen rocks this color. Silver and pink."

"It's the way the sun hits them," Allison said, hopping from one foot to the other. "Damn. It's too hot."

Maggie stepped off the deck into the pebbled beach and started running toward the ocean. "Not if we hurry," she called over her shoulder. But as she got further into the sand, her feet began to burn.

"My god," she cried. "It's like running through coals."

They quickly put on their tennis shoes, unconcerned with how ridiculous they must look wearing their swimsuits and sneakers on a beach where most of the women didn't even bother to wear the top half of their bikinis.

They spread their mats on a little raised plot of beach, far away from the crowds near the veranda and the waiters serving lemonade and champagne.

Look," Allison said. "You'd think Monte Carlo wouldn't need this." She pointed to a huge U.S. Navy aircraft carrier anchored offshore in the distance.

"Why in the world are they here?" Maggie said. "It's not as if we're in a hostile nation."

"Who knows," Allison said. "Maybe the Admiral wanted to see the casinos so they stopped on their way back from wherever they were."

"Let's swim out there," Allison said. "Just to see if we can do it."

"Okay," Maggie said. She ran to the ocean with Allison right behind her. They splashed into the surf and swam out as far as they could before getting tired.

"Oh Ali," Maggie cried, "I can't swim any further." "Okay Maggie," Allison said, "Let's go back."

They turned around and floated back towards the beach; then they rode the waves into the shore when they got close enough to body surf. The rocks crunched beneath their sneakers as they walked back up the beach toward their mats.

They grabbed their towels from their bags, dried off then lay down on their mats, facing away from the Navy ship in order to watch the sunset behind the villas and palm trees.

"This is the life," Allison said.

"Sure is."

Just then two young men came strolling down the beach in plaid swim trunks and high-top tennis shoes. Their milky untanned bodies all but glowed in the amber haze of dusk. Allison nodded at them then said, "Don't look now but we've got visitors."

Maggie pulled a compact from her bag and watched them approach over her shoulder.

"Oh no," she whispered. "They've got dog-tags and matching tattoos."

Both girls giggled.

"Anchors on their biceps, no doubt," Allison said.

"I can't tell what they are from here," Maggie whispered. "Oops, here they come."

"Hello ladies," called one of the sailors.

The girls didn't answer. They waited until the sailors were closer, then they turned around on their mats to face them.

"We just left the Carnival in Nice and we heard there was a great happy hour here at the Plaza each evening. Care to join us?"

Allison tried to think of a diplomatic way to decline, but Maggie said, "Sure, we're staying here overnight but we didn't know about the happy hour."

Allison stiffened. How much information did Maggie feel the need to give to these strangers?

"I'm Andy, and this is Jimmy," he said then reached down and picked up the girl's bags. He slung them both over his right shoulder and said, "Ladies?" holding out his arm as if to escort them.

Maggie stood. "I'm Maggie and this is Ali." She shook hands with Andy and Jimmy, making it extremely awkward for Allison not to do the same.

"Ali?" asked Jimmy. "That's an unusual name."

"It's short for Allison," said Maggie.

"I'm from Cleveland," Andy said, shaking Allison' hand. "Where are you from?"

"Ali and I are from Texas," Maggie said.

"I'm from Topeka," Jimmy said. He took Allison' bag from Andy and reached down to grab her straw mat off the beach. He rolled it up and stuck it in her bag before she could ask him not to.

"May I?" Allison said, taking her cover-up from her bag.

"Crazy thing happened this morning on board," Jimmy said.

"On board?" asked Allison.

"Yeah. We're sailors on that aircraft carrier right there off shore," Jimmy said, pointing to the ship. "One of the planes rolled off. Just like that. Eighty-five million bucks sank down into the ocean."

"Was anyone hurt?" asked Maggie.

"No," Andy said. "Stuff like that happens a lot. You just never hear about it."

"Good," Maggie said. "I don't want to hear about it."

"Why not, Maggie?" asked Allison.

"Because, Ali, I'd rather not know if the Navy is screwing up."

"Yes but don't you think they should be a little more careful? I mean if a corporation lost eighty-five million dollars by letting a plane sink into the ocean, don't you think there'd be some accountability?"

"That depends on what company it is," said Andy. "Anyway, who wants a beer?"

"I do," Maggie said.

"I'll take lemonade," said Allison, sitting down in a chaise lounge. Jimmy sat down beside her. He reached in his pocket, pulled out a few bills and gave them to Andy. "I'll take a beer," he said.

"Come with me," said Andy.

Jimmy hesitated and then winked at Allison.

Andy and Jimmy went to the veranda bar and ordered their drinks.

Maggie sat down on the edge of the chaise lounge next to Allison.

"Are you hungry, Ali?"

Allison leaned in close to Maggie and whispered, "Hungry for some real conversation. These guys are boring me to tears."

"So they're just fake guys to you? They're not real?"

Allison shrugged. "Not exactly what I expected to meet on a beach in Monte Carlo."

"Oh," Maggie sighed. "I guess I see what you mean."

Just then Andy and Jimmy returned with their drinks. Andy reached in his pocket and grabbed a set of pink plastic Mardi Gras beads. "I won them in Nice," he said. "At the carnival."

He gave them to Maggie.

Jimmy pulled a set of Mardi Gras beads from his pocket. He reached out to Allison and slipped them over her head. She removed her sunglasses so the beads could slip down into place around her neck, but as she did, her hand brushed against Jimmy's hand.

At that moment she felt a bolt of electricity race up her arm and into her body as if she'd touched an electrical outlet and gotten shocked.

"Woa," she said. "Did you feel that?"

Jimmy nodded and smiled then adjusted the beads around her neck.

"Thank you," Allison said, and took a sip of her lemonade.

"You're quite welcome, said Jimmy. "This is a great beach, isn't it?"

Maggie nodded. Allison touched her fingertips lightly against the plastic beads around her neck. "It's nothing compared to the beaches in South Texas, especially Padre Island."

"Is that a fact?" asked Andy.

"Yes," said Allison. "The sand back home is creamy white and soft as baby powder. And there's palm trees and a perpetual warm breeze. And there's no rocks on the beach like this stuff here. I can hardly stand to walk on it."

"You like living in Texas?" asked Andy.

"Sometimes," said Allison.

"I don't," said Maggie. "I want to live in New York."

Jimmy laughed and took a sip of his beer.

"What's funny about that?" asked Maggie.

"Nothing," said Jimmy. "I was just thinking of something one of my college professors said about New York. He called it a thinking man's cesspool."

"A thinking man?" retorted Allison. "And I suppose this two bit professor at some Podunk college in Kansas has every right to criticize New York since he's probably never even been there."

"Not true," said Jimmy. "He graduated from NYU, and got his PhD from Columbia. So I'm sure he has valid reasons for not liking New York."

"Does he like Topeka better?" asked Maggie sincerely. "Maybe he's from a small town and finds New York over-stimulating or something like that."

Andy raised his beer to Maggie then said, "Here's to the peacemaker, I drink to your spirit of camaraderie among strangers." Andy took a drink of his beer then Jimmy raised his bottle and took a drink.

"To peacemakers," said Jimmy, and took another sip.

"Do you consider yourselves peacemakers?" asked Maggie.

"Or warmongers?" asked Allison.

Jimmy smiled.

Andy didn't.

Allison could see the flush in Andy's cheeks as he tried to hide his anger.

"We are U.S. Navy fighter pilots. We are en route to Basra, Iraq where we will try to facilitate peace for a nation in chaos," replied Andy coolly.

Allison could see she was getting to him. But Jimmy was another matter. He seemed calm and unruffled.

"My professor, the thinking man from New York, is dean of the Washburn University School of Law. And he is a fantastic educator."

"Did you graduate, or drop out to go to war?" asked Allison.

"I graduated Summa Cum Laude from Washburn with an undergraduate degree in Political Science."

"What about you?" Maggie asked Andy.

"I've never been to college. My old man is a carpenter in Cleveland and he wanted me to take over his business. But I wanted to get out of Cleveland and do something different with my life. I intend to study law after I finish my tour of duty."

"*If* you finish it," said Allison.

Andy and Jimmy exchanged glances.

"What Ali means is that Iraq isn't exactly the safest place for an American to be at the moment."

"We're aware that war is dangerous," replied Andy. "But we took an oath to serve our country and that's what we're planning to do."

"Do you really think the United States will be "served" if you're killed in action?" asked Allison.

"What are you doing with your life that is so much more meaningful than that of a soldier?" asked Andy.

"Everyone finds meaning in different ways, especially if they're from places that are worlds apart," said Maggie. "And if you think about it, Americans are not all that different from Iraqis."

Andy took another sip of his beer watching Maggie as she spoke.

"In fact," Maggie continued, "One of my psychology professors said there are five different needs that everyone on the planet has in common."

"Even if you're from Afghanistan or Iraq?" asked Jimmy.

"Yes," said Maggie. "First is the need to love and be loved. Second is the need to belong. Third is the need to achieve. Fourth is the need for security – material, emotional, and spiritual." Maggie took another sip of her drink.

"What's the fifth need?" asked Andy.

"I can't remember," said Maggie. She smiled, and blushed a bit.

"I'd say the need for finding beauty is a big need that all humans have in common," said Allison.

"Finding beauty?" laughed Jimmy. "Do you really think the average citizen in rural Iraq wakes up each day hoping to find beauty?"

Allison cocked her head at Jimmy, narrowing her eyes. "I think everyone longs for beauty, whether you're from Hollywood, or rural Iraq. You just go about it in different ways, depending on your culture."

"I don't consciously seek out beauty," said Andy. "I wake up and focus all my concentration on succeeding in my maneuvers. But searching for beauty isn't even on my list of things to do each day."

"Figures," said Allison and smiled curtly at Andy. "I truly believe that if you don't search for beauty you won't ever find it."

"Or worse yet," said Jimmy, "What if you're so busy searching for beauty that you don't recognize it when it's staring you in the face." He motioned at himself and at Andy. Maggie laughed.

"Are you implying that I'm failing to recognize beauty right in front of my face?" demanded Allison.

"Yes. I am. Andy and I are beautiful and you are being combative and failing to see our true inner beauty." He then batted his eyes.

Everyone laughed. Even Allison.

"Okay," said Allison. "Impress me, show me your beauty."

"Fine," said Jimmy. He cleared his throat and closed his eyes. Then he said, "I will recite a poem for you that I had to memorize in high school. I still remember it to this day because it is so damn beautiful. Here goes:

> for marilyn m.
> slipping keenly into bright ashes
> target of vanilla tears
> your sure body lit candles for men
> on dark nights,
> and now your night is darker
> than the candle's reach
> and we will forget you, somewhat,
> and it is not kind
> but real bodies are nearer
> and as the worms pant for your bones,
> I would so like to tell you
> that this happens to bears and elephants
> to tyrants and heroes and ants
> and frogs,
> still, you brought us something,
> some type of small victory,

and for this I say: good
and let us grieve no more;
like a flower dried and thrown away,
we forget, we remember,
we wait. child, child, child,
I raise my drink a full minute
and smile.

Jimmy raised his beer to his lips and took a sip.

Maggie said, "That's awesome. Who wrote it?"

"Charles Bukowski," said Jimmy.

"You read Bukowski in high school?" asked Maggie.

"It was an honors class on 20th Century American Literature."

"What do you want to be when you grow up?" asked Allison, "I mean, when you finish being a sailor."

"An attorney," said Jimmy.

"Same as me," said Andy. "What about you? What are you planning to do with your life?"

Allison shrugged. "I haven't decided yet. I thought seeing the world a bit would help broaden my horizons."

"Tell us another poem," said Maggie.

"Sorry," said Jimmy. "That's all I know."

"I don't believe you," said Allison. "You're just being shy."

"Oh enough of this idle palaver," said Jimmy. "Let's do something. Are you guys hungry?"

Allison shrugged. Maggie shook her head.

"Let's take a walk down the beach," suggested Jimmy.

Allison stood. "I'd like to see some of the sights here. Maybe see the casinos or the royal palace. Have you seen Princess Grace's palace?"

"Who's Princess Grace?" asked Jimmy.

Andy laughed.

"Are you serious?" asked Maggie. "You don't know who Princess Grace is?"

"Of course I know who Grace Kelly is, I was making a joke."

"How long are you guys going to be here in Monte Carlo?" asked Maggie.

"Today and tomorrow," said Jimmy.

"Let's do some sightseeing tomorrow," said Allison. "I'm tired. It's been a long day."

Jimmy sighed. "I'm afraid we're losing them," he said to Andy, who smiled then finished the last of his beer.

"What's wrong Andy?" asked Jimmy, "Why are you so reticent?"

"I'm waiting for you to get Allison's cell number so you can hook up later tonight or tomorrow."

Everyone laughed.

"713-448-6244," said Maggie. "We're in room 1101 here at the Plaza. I don't know how long we'll be staying here, but we'll be here tomorrow if you want to do some sight seeing. Give us a call."

"Sounds good to me," Jimmy said, standing up. He took his cell phone from his pocket and entered Allison' number. He held his hand out to Allison. "Let's meet on the terrace tomorrow for coffee, say 10:30? Is that too early?"

Maggie laughed. "Sounds good to me." She reached out to Andy to shake his hand. "We'll see you tomorrow."

Allison and Maggie went back to their room and lay down to take a short nap before getting ready for dinner. At 8:00 that evening they went downstairs to the dining room and ordered steak and lobster with champagne. While they were eating dinner a gentleman wearing a white dinner jacket and a turban approached their table.

"Would you ladies be so kind as to accept an invitation to accompany myself and my friend to the Casino Monte-Carlo after you finish your dinner?"

He wore a diamond stud in each ear and a gold Rolex on his wrist. Allison noticed a small scar on his left cheek, and then noticed a faint smell of almonds which was not altogether unpleasant.

"Where is your friend?" asked Maggie, glancing around the dining room.

"He is dining in his rooms upstairs. He dislikes eating among strangers."

"I see," said Allison, "But he doesn't mind gambling with strangers?"

"I beg your pardon?" said the man.

"You invited us to accompany you to the Casino, but we're strangers."

"Yes but it is my friend's custom, and it has brought him much luck at the roulette table in the past. Please grant us the pleasure of your company." He smiled, revealing perfectly straight and extraordinarily white teeth.

Maggie smiled. "We'd be delighted to go with you. We'll be through eating in about twenty minutes."

"Good. My name is Mizrah, and we will meet you in the front lobby in say half an hour?" He looked at his watch then said, "Make that forty-five minutes."

The girls agreed then watched in silence as Mizrah made his way out of the dining room back to the lobby.

"Are you sure you want to go with them?" asked Allison.

"Why not?" said Maggie.

"Well, they could turn out to be perverts or criminals, you never can tell."

"I think we'll be safe, there are lots of people around. As long as we're in a crowd what harm could it do?"

Allison sipped her champagne and dabbed the linen napkin at her lips. "I wonder if we'll bump into those sailors?" she said.

"They don't seem like the Casino types," said Maggie. "Besides, I doubt they have a jacket and tie and I read in the guide book that the Casino Monte-Carlo requires men to wear a jacket and tie."

"You're probably right about that."

The girls finished their dinner then went back to their room to brush their teeth and put on fresh lipstick. When they came back to the lobby, Mizrah and his friend were waiting by the elevator. Mizrah waved.

"Hello ladies. This is my friend Omar."

"I'm Allison."

"And I'm Maggie."

"Lovely to meet you both," said Omar. "We saw you earlier on the beach and thought you would bring us luck if you came to the gaming tables with us."

"Come this way," said Mizrah. "The car is waiting."

They stepped outside into the cool night air and a white Rolls Royce pulled up to meet them. They all got in the car and rode the few blocks to the Casino Monte-Carlo. As they got out of the car, Allison gazed up at the gilded bas-relief sculpted arches adorning the grand entrance of the Casino.

They walked up the steps and passed several elegant fountains with golden lights and gilded statues surrounding them. They entered the atrium, tiled in shimmering marble and lined with several marble columns leading up to the casino proper which had many ornate baroque frescoes and sculptures. As they entered the casino an usher welcomed Omar and Mizrah, and called them by name.

"The usual?" asked the usher.

"Yes please," replied Omar.

Allison glanced around at the multitude of red and gold decorations. The walls were covered with intricate stained glass windows and adorned with bronze sconces and lamps. The entire room seemed to shimmer with opulence and luxury.

The usher returned with a leather-covered box of chips for Omar and Mizrah.

"Ladies?" said Omar, as he held his arm out for Maggie. She took his arm and he led her into the roulette gaming room.

On his first bet, Omar won $5,000. Maggie and Allison were stunned.

"You see?" laughed Omar, "You bring me luck."

Omar and Mizrah continued to win for the next two hours. Allison wondered if Omar was a little bit psychic in order to know which number and color to bet on so successfully.

After two hours of steady winning, Omar cashed in his chips and announced that he wished to stop while his luck held.

"Would you like to accompany us to the Living Room for a drink?"

"What's the Living Room?" asked Maggie.

"It's a nightclub. It's very chic. You'll like it. Americans always like it."

"Where are you from?" asked Allison.

"Beirut," said Omar. "And Mizrah is from Syria. We met while we were in university together in London."

"What did you study in college?" asked Allison.

"You're very inquisitive, aren't you?" said Omar.

They left the Casino and hurried down the steps to their waiting white Rolls.

Omar told the driver to take them to Le Living Room and then turned to Allison.

"I studied international business and economics," he said. "Mizrah did as well. We had several classes together."

"Have you ever been to America?" asked Maggie.

Omar laughed. "I visited my father in New York when I was a child, but I found it a little too hostile."

Allison laughed. "You're from the Middle East but you find America too hostile?"

Omar nodded. "There's so much crime and poverty."

"What about suicide bombers and the refugee camps on the Gaza Strip?"

"Touché," said Omar. He tugged at his tie then said, "Perhaps violence and poverty is a given in our world today."

"But it doesn't have to be," said Maggie. "There is enough money and food to clothe, house and feed everyone on this planet."

Mizrah smiled and took Maggie's hand. "You are very idealistic," he said. "I'm afraid you look at the world through glasses of rose."

Maggie and Allison exchanged glances.

The driver pulled up to the curb and a valet opened the car door. They got out and entered the Living Room without waiting in line. Once inside Allison was surprised to find the entire bar comprised of a series of little alcoves, each furnished with overstuffed Queen Ann high back chairs and couches. There were bookshelves and reading lamps everywhere. It was indeed a series of tiny living rooms. Allison liked the feel of the bar.

"It's very European," opined Allison.

Omar laughed.

Mizrah glanced around and said, "How so?"

"Well for starters," said Allison. "You won't find bookshelves filled with books like this in any nightclub in the U.S., no matter how chic the club."

"Let's sit here," said Omar as they approached an empty couch. He waved to a waiter and held up four fingers. The waiter waved back then hurried off to the bar. When the waiter returned he was carrying an ice bucket with a bottle of Champagne and four glasses. He set the bucket down on the coffee table in front of the couch and poured a glass for Omar to taste. He nodded then the waiter finished pouring the Champagne.

"A toast," said Omar as he raised his glass. "To our new good luck charms." He leaned over and touched his glass to Allison' glass and looked deep into her eyes.

Just then a man's hand reached down onto Allison' shoulder and she looked up to find Jimmy, the sailor, standing behind the couch.

"Fancy meeting you here!" he said, laughing. "Would you care to dance?"

Allison glanced at Omar, then at Maggie, who nodded as if to say 'go ahead, I'll wait here while you go have some fun.'

Allison put her Champagne flute down on the coffee table then said to Omar, "Please excuse me, I'll be right back."

Omar gazed after Allison and Jimmy as they headed out to the dance floor. He watched them dance and did not engage in the conversation that Maggie was trying so hard to facilitate.

From the dance floor Allison could see Maggie laughing and talking to Mizrah. Then Jimmy put his arms around her and kissed her on the forehead. She put her arms around his back and could feel him sweating underneath his silk Hawaiian shirt. He looked so much like a tourist, but he was being extremely charming and making Allison laugh with his off beat sense of humor.

After forty-five minutes, Allison said she was tired and wanted to sit down. When Jimmy and Allison returned to the couch they found Maggie sitting alone.

"Where's Hadji and Johnny Quest?" asked Jimmy.

Maggie laughed. "They said American girls, as a rule, have very little class. Then they left."

"That's right," said Jimmy. "That's why American guys love them so much."

Allison laughed. "You are a rare find."

Jimmy gazed at Allison, grinning. "What do you mean?"

"Well it's rare to find someone so completely lacking in class, who freely admits it, and who can also quote Bukowski."

"I can quote a plethora of writers," he said. He reached for the Champagne bottle but it was empty.

"Let's go somewhere else," he said.

"Where's Andy?" asked Maggie.

"He's at a Houka bar around the corner."

"Oh let's go there!" said Maggie. "I've been wanting to try that. We've seen several Houka bars here along the coast."

"Okay. We're on a mission," he said. "To find Andy and let Maggie experience Houka."

As they were leaving the bar, the waiter hurried up behind them and asked them to pay the bill. Omar and Mizrah had left instructions with the waiter that the ladies were responsible for the bill.

Jimmy laughed. "And he said Americans have no class."

He took a wad of cash from his pocket and paid the waiter. Then they hurried out of the Living Room and back into the street. It was quiet outside after being inundated with such loud dance music.

They walked down the street, linking arms, with Jimmy in the middle between Allison and Maggie. They were laughing and enjoying the cool breeze off the harbor. When they reached Café Paris, they found Andy sitting alone, sucking on a Houka water pipe. He was fairly drunk and didn't recognize them immediately.

"Hey sailor, wanna get lucky?" asked Maggie as she sat down beside him. "I'll have whatever he's drinking."

Jimmy picked up Andy's bottle and read the label. "Framboise. Raspberry Lambic Ale."

"It's imported," said Andy. "From Belgium."

"So it is," said Jimmy. He went up to the bar and ordered three more lambic ales. When he returned to their table, he found Maggie and Allison sharing the water pipe with Andy. When he set the bottles of ale down on the table beside the water pipe, Allison looked up at Jimmy and said, "Maybe I should ask him instead, he talks more than Andy does."

"Ask me what?" said Jimmy as he sat down next to Allison.

"Aren't you afraid you could be killed?"

"Everyone dies," said Jimmy, sipping his ale.

"That's true," said Allison, "But volunteering to put yourself in harms way certainly heightens the risk of one's imminent demise."

Jimmy laughed, then reached over and took a hit off the water pipe.

"A very learned man once said, 'Do the thing that you are afraid to do, and the death of fear is certain'."

"Or the death of yourself more likely," said Allison.

"Who said that?" asked Maggie.

"Ralph Waldo Emerson," said Jimmy.

Allison laughed. "So you not only recite Bukowski, you can quote Emerson as well. Yet you still want to go to war. It just doesn't make any sense to me."

Jimmy smiled and set his bottle of ale down on the table. "I know there's a very real chance we won't be coming back home," he said. "But that doesn't keep me from going. I believe wholeheartedly in our nation and our quest to rid the world of terrorism."

"But the war in Iraq is about oil. And defense contractors. Companies like Halliburton and Schlumberger are getting all those big fat government contracts."

Jimmy reached for the water pipe and took a long slow drag on the nozzle. He looked at Allison then blew smoke out of each side of his mouth.

"You sound like my father," said Andy. "He hated President Bush and the way we got into the war, and he's angry as hell at me for enlisting."

"What can I say to you to make you change your mind?" asked Allison.

Jimmy looked at her and said, "I'm pregnant."

No one laughed.

"That was a joke," said Jimmy, grinning widely.

Andy looked at his watch. "God, I'm tired. I'm going back to the ship. You coming?"

Jimmy winked at Allison. She pretended she didn't notice as she reached for the water pipe. She took a long slow pull from the pipe and felt the calming effect as the tobacco smoke filled her lungs.

Maggie looked at her watch. "It's late," she said. "If we're meeting on the terrace at 10:30 in the morning, we should all turn in."

Jimmy reached across the table and took Allison' hand. "Can we walk you back to your hotel?" He stared into her eyes then lifted her hand to his lips and kissed the back of her hand.

Returning his gaze, Allison lifted Jimmy's hand to her lips and kissed his hand. He smiled at her as she lifted his fingers to her lips and kissed each of his fingertips then gently began to suck on his third finger.

Jimmy closed his eyes and leaned his head back,

"I think I could go AWOL for you," he said.

Andy got up and said, "I'm leaving."

Maggie stood and said, "Please walk me back to my hotel."

Andy shrugged then held his arm out for Maggie. She took his arm and they headed down the street back towards the Plaza Hotel.

Jimmy leaned in and kissed Allison on the lips. She kissed him back, her tongue gently finding his. He put his hands on her shoulders and squeezed her then pushed her away.

He took a deep breath then said, "Run away with me."

She laughed, then looked into his eyes and could see he wasn't joking.

"You can't just run away, can you?" she asked. "Won't they come looking for you and put you in a military prison?"

He leaned towards her and kissed her again. She closed her eyes and kissed him back, thinking about running away. Then she opened her eyes.

"You're leaving tomorrow, aren't you?" she asked.

"Tomorrow night at 11:00 pm. We've got all day to be together. I'll take you to the Royal Palace and show you the sites."

"What about right now?" she said, lifting his arm and putting it around her shoulder.

"I doubt the palace is open now," he said.

"I didn't mean that."

"What did you mean?"

She stared at him, searching his face for some sort of sign, some glimmer of what he would look like in twenty years, or some shadow of what his children would look like in ten years. She put her hands on either side of his face and pulled him closer to her.

"You should never have joined the Navy," she said.

He laughed. "That is absolutely not true. It's probably the smartest thing I've ever done."

She frowned.

"How else would I have ever met you?"

Her frown relaxed. Then she closed her eyes.

He leaned his head down next to hers and kissed her on the neck. She leaned her head to one side, allowing him greater access. He kissed her neck again then put his hand on the small of her back.

She immediately arched her back and he kissed her mouth. Then she pushed him away and stood up.

"Let's get a room and spend all night together."

"Excellent idea," said Jimmy.

He put his arm around her and they walked down the street back towards the Plaza Hotel. Two blocks down they turned the corner and headed half a block away from the beach until they reached a column of neon blue palm trees.

"Oh it's lovely! Let's stay here," Allison said.

They walked up the steps and past several neon palm trees and they entered the hotel. It had a blue neon sign above the door that read "Blue Palms Inn."

Jimmy took Allison by the arm and led her to a couch in the lobby.

"Wait here," he said. "I'll be right back."

He approached the front desk and rang the bell. A yawning clerk stepped around from the back room and smoothed his hair and straightened his tie.

Jimmy took the wad of cash from his pocket and paid for the room. He then waited for the clerk to leave the front desk then he approached Allison.

"I got a room with a view," he said.

She smiled.

"Room 311. Third floor," he said. "He said you can see the beach from the balcony."

They rode the elevator in silence, until Jimmy reached down and licked the back of Allison' neck. She immediately reached over and grabbed his crotch. He took her hands, turned her around and kissed her firmly on the lips.

The elevator stopped and the doors opened. They hurried down the hall to room 311. Jimmy unlocked the door and pushed the door open wide. He then picked Allison up and carried her inside.

"Hey what are you doing?" she said.

He laughed and kicked the door shut behind him. He carried her to the king size bed and laid her down gently. He then crawled on top of her and began kissing her lips, her neck, her chest.

Hours passed as they made love with the window open, listening to the surf hit the beach a couple blocks away as the wind silently stirred the curtains. Suddenly Allison pushed Jimmy away and wiped a tear from her face.

"Hey. What's wrong?" he whispered.

She looked at him them rolled over, facing away from him.

He stroked her hair and the back of her neck.

"What is it?" he said.

"I may never see you again," she said then pulled the covers up over her bare shoulder.

Jimmy got up and poured himself a glass of water. He walked over to the balcony and stood there looking out at the sea. He could see the lights on his ship moored off shore. He gazed at the ship for a moment, then went to the desk and scribbled something on the hotel stationery. He sat down beside Allison.

"Here's my address on board ship, and my parent's address in Topeka. They'll never move so you'll always be able to reach me through them."

She took the paper from him and folded it up and put it in her purse on the bedside table.

"Tell me another poem," she said.

Jimmy leaned back against the headboard and draped his arm over her shoulder. He caressed her shoulder gently as he spoke.

"This one is called "The Paper on the Floor," and it is by Bukowski as well. Here goes:

I can see the comic section folded in half,
I can see the black and white lines
and some faces I don't care to discern;
but a thin illness overcomes me
at the sight of this portion of paper
and I look away
and try not to think

that much of our living life
is true to the little paper faces
that stare up from our feet
and grin and jump and gesture,
to be wrapped in tomorrow's garbage
and thrown away."

Allison snuggled up against Jimmy, leaning her head on his shoulder.

"That's lovely and sad," she said. "Just like how I feel right now."

"Lovely and sad?" asked Jimmy.

She nodded. "Is Bukowski talking about the obituary section?"

"Most likely," he said.

"It's funny how fast our lives come and go," she said.

He nodded. "I didn't mean to make you sad," he said.

She glanced up at him then shut her eyes. "I wish tomorrow would never come."

He took her hand in his and kissed her fingertips.

"Tomorrow I will take you to the Royal Palace and show you the sites of Monte Carlo."

"Then you'll get on your ship and sail out of my life forever."

He took her face in his hands and stared into her eyes. "I gave you my address, we can keep in touch and after my tour of duty is up, I'll come to Texas and find you."

She shook her head, fighting back tears then forced a little laugh.

He didn't laugh. He said, "What makes you so sure I won't come back from Iraq?"

She pushed him away then stood up in front of him.

"What makes you so sure you will?" she said then she went out the open sliding glass door onto the balcony.

A crescent moon hung high overhead. She sat down on the chaise lounge and stared up at the sky. A cool wind blew, tinkling a wind chime on the balcony of the high-rise condominium building next door. Jimmy came outside onto the balcony wrapped in the bed sheet. He sat down next to Allison and draped the sheet over her body.

They sat in silence on the chaise lounge watching the moon over the Mediterranean. They fell asleep side by side.

Nine months later, Allison was working as a copywriter for a large advertising agency in Dallas when she received a certified letter from Mr. and Mrs. James D. Whitmore, from Topeka, Kansas stating that their son, Jimmy, had been severely injured in Iraq and had been flown to the Veterans Hospital in Palo Alto, California where he was receiving physical therapy. The letter did not state the nature of his injury; it merely said it was severe.

Allison was shocked. No wonder he had stopped writing to her. She wanted to call him immediately, but decided against it. It would be difficult to judge his reaction on the phone. She thought it best to see him in person.

The next day, Allison took a few days off from work and booked a flight to the SFO airport. When she arrived, she rented a car then drove straight to Palo Alto to the Veterans Hospital.

When she found Jimmy, he was sitting in a wheelchair in his room, working a crossword puzzle.

She knocked on the partially open door.

"Hello?" she said, stepping into the room

Jimmy looked up and smiled immediately when he saw her. "Aren't you a sight for sore eyes!"

She entered the room and approached him. She bent down and kissed him on the cheek.

"How did you find me?" he asked.

"I wrote to your parents."

He folded the crossword puzzle magazine and tossed it onto the bedside table.

"They just left here last week. They were here for two weeks. And I'm afraid I wasn't very hospitable towards the end of their visit."

"What happened?" she asked. "Did your plane get shot down?"

"Nothing so valiant, I'm afraid," he said, adjusting the blanket covering his thighs. "I was walking down the street in Basra and a car bomb went off in front of me."

"You could've been killed," she whispered.

"I know. I'm lucky to be alive," he said. "Even though I'm missing both legs below the knee and three fingers on my left hand."

"At least you're not left handed," she said.

"That's right, from the eternal optimist."

"I've been so worried, you stopped writing me three months ago," she said.

"I know, but I've been a little busy. I've had six surgeries and ten weeks of physical therapy."

"I wrote to your parents and told them who I was and that we had met in Monte Carlo. They wrote me back and told me you were here. I didn't ask them if they thought it would be okay for me to visit. I just hopped on a plane and here I am. I hope you don't mind."

"Mind? Hell I'm delighted to see you. I just wish I wasn't in such a pathetic situation. The doctors say I probably won't walk again, but I'm scheduled to receive new prosthetic legs in three weeks, and then I'll start walking on my own. I'll show them." He slammed his fist down on the armrest of his wheelchair.

Allison shifted her weight. "Maybe I should have waited before coming out here to see you."

He glanced up at her then looked down at the floor. "I'm sorry," he said. "I just get so angry sometimes."

"That's understandable," she said.

"I was a fool to enlist," he said. "I was brash and arrogant."

Allison stepped up beside him and took his hand in hers then she kissed the back of his hand.

He looked away.

"Do you want to get out of this place, maybe get some lunch or go see a movie?"

He shook his head. "Maybe tomorrow."

She sat down on the bed next to his wheelchair, still holding his hand.

"How long are you planning to stay?" he asked.

"I booked a flight out in four days, but I can always change it if you want me to stay longer."

"Let's take it one day at a time," he said.

They sat in silence for a few moments, each one lost in their own thoughts.

Allison closed her eyes and imagined them together in the Blue Palms Inn. She smiled as she thought about the wind chime on the balcony next door and the breeze stirring the curtains in the open window.

Then she remembered the book she had brought for Jimmy. "I almost forgot," she said, reaching into her bag. She pulled out a book wrapped in brown paper with a red ribbon tied around it.

"What's this?" he asked, smiling.

"Just a little something to keep your mind occupied when you're not doing crossword puzzles, that is."

He untied the ribbon then pulled the wrapping paper off. He opened the book and flipped through several pages.

"This is just great," he said, smiling at Allison.

He held up the book, the collected poems of Ralph Waldo Emerson, and then put it down in his lap.

"I shouldn't have stopped writing to you after the accident, but I couldn't stand to think of myself as a cripple, and I didn't want you to see me out of pity."

"Didn't you read any of my letters?" she asked.

He looked down at the book in his lap. "Yes I read them, many times. I just couldn't bring myself to answer them."

"Well if you read them then you know that it isn't pity that I feel for you."

"Why?" he asked then looked up at her. He stared her right in the eye. "I mean we're practically strangers, why is there anything else that would motivate you?"

"Because," she said as she stood up and moved right up next to him. She took his hands and knelt down in front of his wheelchair. "Because you make me laugh, and you quote poetry, and you're a fantastic kisser. What more does a girl need to fall in love?"

He glanced at her then pulled his hands back away from her. He put his hands on his wheels and pushed himself away from her. He wheeled himself over in front of the window then opened the curtains and the blinds.

"In love?" he said, facing out the window.

"I could move here and find a job then we could be together every day."

He laughed. "What about when they finally release me? Then what?"

"I'll go wherever you go."

"Even if it's Podunk, Kansas?" he asked.

"Anywhere. That's why I came here, to tell you in person."

He turned his wheelchair around to face her. "You'd do that for me?"

"For us," she said. Then she stood and walked up to him. She bent down and put her arms around him and whispered into his ear.

"Remember the Blue Palms?"

He smiled.

"It could be that way again," she said. She kissed him gently on the cheek. "Just give it a chance."

"You'd really move here just to be with me while I learn to walk again?"

"Stanford University is in Palo Alto, isn't it? Maybe I could get a job there."

He smiled. "We had a great time in Monte Carlo, didn't we?"
"It could be like that for the rest of our lives," she said, stroking his cheek. She kissed him on the lips. He pulled away.

"What if it doesn't work out?" he said. "What if you quit your job and move here, and it doesn't work out between us? Then what?"

"But it will work," she said standing up. "If you just give it a chance."

He sighed. "I'm sorry I'm not in better spirits."

"Don't apologize for your anger. Use it to help you focus on learning how to walk again."

Jimmy laughed. "You sound like Yoda. 'To make yourself stronger, young Skywalker, your anger you must use.'"

Allison laughed. "You could go to law school here in California. Then you could start studying for the Bar Exam. Then we could move to San Francisco and live in an old Victorian home with a view of the bay from our living room window. And when you're ready, we can have a family."

He laughed. "You've got it all figured out, haven't you."

"Yes I do," she said, crossing her arms over her chest. "I've had plenty of time to think about it."

He reached up and touched her strawberry blond hair. "Berkeley has an awesome law school," he said.

"So does Stanford." She leaned her forehead down and touched it to his forehead.

"We can make this work," she said then kissed him on the lips.

He kissed her back.

"I'm going to go look for a newspaper so I can check out the classifieds, to see what's available here."

As she headed for the door he said, "Wait."

She stopped at the door and turned back to face him.

"I just want you to know that I won't be tied to a fucking wheelchair for the rest of my life."

She smiled. "I know that Jimmy. I'll be back in a few minutes."

She pulled the door closed behind her as she left the room.

Jimmy picked up his Emerson book and thumbed trough the pages stopping on page 311, he put his finger down on a random verse and read:

> And I am here
> On the green earth contemplating the moon
> Much marveling what may betide tomorrow
> I love my life.

Jimmy dog-eared the page and put the book down on the bedside table. He gazed out the window at the parking lot below and saw Allison walking out to get in her car. As he watched her drive off, he gripped the wheels on his chair, squeezing the rubber against the rim. He then wheeled himself back to his desk, took out his journal and copied down the verse from page 311, "And I am here on the green earth contemplating the moon…"

He hesitated then glanced at himself in the mirror. His face was thinner now and his cheekbones were more pronounced since the accident. He continued writing, "Much marveling what may betide tomorrow. I love my life."

Then he wrote, "I will do whatever it takes to get to that place again where I love my life."

He put the journal away, then wheeled himself down the hallway to the exercise room, determined not to waste another minute without working towards his ultimate goal of building back his strength and learning to walk again.

ABOUT THE AUTHOR

A new shining star in the literary world has emerged. Melissa L. White, a Houston, Texas native, now lives and writes in the San Francisco Bay area. Her literary fiction is almost poetic, as witnessed in her debut collection of short fiction, "On the Green Earth Contemplating the Moon." This book reflects her passion for stories that remind you that no matter how harsh the circumstances, and no matter how bitter the reality, life is beautiful and we are all lucky to be a part of the shared human experience. She writes with compassion, hope, and a pervasive theme that something good is just around the corner. She is a gifted story teller whose work begs to be read. She is currently at work on her next book of short fiction as well on a major non-fiction book with co-author, Terrence Brejla.

Melissa is most influenced by Ernest Hemingway, F. Scott Fitzgerald, Flannery O'Connor, Raymond Carver, Jean Rhys, Ray Bradbury, and Anthony Doerr. She adheres to the tenant that Isabel Allende was driving at when she said, "Write what should not be forgotten." Most of Melissa's fiction is loosely based on personal experience, or some derivation thereof, and she firmly believes in following the painter Georgia O'Keeffe's advice when she said, "Art is about making the unknown known." And this knowing is what fills Melissa's fiction with insights into life, spirituality, and the human condition.

www.ingramcontent.com/pod-product-compliance
Lightning Source LLC
Chambersburg PA
CBHW030639130626
46552CB00002B/937